What It Means to Be a Libertarian

ALSO BY CHARLES MURRAY

Losing Ground: American Social Policy 1950–1980

In Pursuit: Of Happiness and Good Government

The Bell Curve: Intelligence and Class Structure in American Life
(with Richard J. Herrnstein)

What It
MEANS
to Be a
LIBERTARIAN

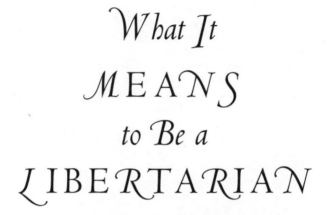

A PERSONAL
INTERPRETATION

CHARLES
MURRAY

BROADWAY BOOKS

New York

Broadway Books titles may be purchased for business or promotional use or for special sales. For information, please write to: Special Markets Department, Bantam Doubleday Dell Publishing Group, Inc., 1540 Broadway, New York, NY 10036.

BROADWAY BOOKS and its logo, a letter B bisected on the diagonal, are trademarks of Broadway Books, a division of Bantam Doubleday Dell Publishing Group, Inc.

FIRST EDITION

Designed by Marysarah Quinn

Library of Congress Cataloging-in-Publication Data
Murray, Charles A.
    What it means to be a libertarian : a personal interpretation / Charles Murray. — 1st ed.
        p.   cm.
    Includes bibliographical references.
    ISBN 0-553-06928-4
    1. Libertarianism.   I. Title.
JC585.M885   1997
320.5′12—dc20   96-33531
                                                              CIP

97   98   99   00   10   9   8   7   6   5   4   3   2   1

*To the memory of my friends Richard Herrnstein and Karl Hess,
as different as two men could be except in their courage,
kindness, and wisdom.*

Contents

Let us, then, with courage and confidence pursue our own federal and republican principles, our attachment to our union and representative government. . . . Entertaining a due sense of our equal right to the use of our own faculties, to the acquisitions of our industry, to honor and confidence from our fellow citizens, resulting not from birth but from our actions and their sense of them; enlightened by a benign religion, professed, indeed, and practiced in various forms, yet all of them including honesty, truth, temperance, gratitude, and the love of man; acknowledging and adoring an overruling Providence, which by all its dispensations proves that it delights in the happiness of man here and his greater happiness hereafter; with all these blessings, what more is necessary to make us a happy and prosperous people? Still one thing more, fellow citizens—a wise and frugal government, which shall restrain men from injuring one another, which shall leave them otherwise free to regulate their own pursuits of industry and improvement, and shall not take from the mouth of labor the bread it has earned. This is the sum of good government, and this is necessary to close the circle of our felicities.

THOMAS JEFFERSON
First Inaugural Address
March 4, 1801

INTRODUCTION

IN THE LAST QUARTER of the eighteenth century the American Founders created a society based on the belief that human happiness is intimately connected with personal freedom and responsibility. The twin pillars of the system they created were limits on the power of the central government and protection of individual rights.

A few people, of whom I am one, think that the Founders' insights are as true today as they were two centuries ago. We believe that human happiness requires freedom and that freedom requires limited government. Limited government means a very small one, shorn of almost all of the apparatus we have come to take for granted during the last sixty years.

Most people are baffled by such views. Don't we realize that this is postindustrial America, not Jefferson's agrarian society? Don't we realize that without big government millions of the elderly would be destitute, corporations would destroy the environment, and employers would be free once more to exploit their workers? Where do we suppose blacks would be if it weren't for the government? Women? Haven't we noticed that America has huge social problems that aren't going to be dealt with unless the government does something about them?

This book tries to explain how we can believe that the less government, the better. Why a society run on the principles of limited government would advance human happiness. How such a society would lead to greater individual fulfillment, more vital communities, a richer culture. Why such a society would contain fewer poor people, fewer neglected children, fewer criminals. How such a society would not abandon the less fortunate but would care for them better than does the society we have now.

Many books address the historical, economic, sociological, philosophical, and constitutional issues raised in these pages. A bibliographic essay at the end of the book points you to some of the basic sources, but the book you are about to read contains no footnotes. It has no tables and but a single graph. My purpose is not to provide proofs but to explain a way of looking at the world.

A Note About the Way This Book Uses the Word Libertarian

The correct word for my view of the world is *liberal.* "Liberal" is the simplest anglicization of the Latin *liber,* and freedom is what classical liberalism is all about. The writers of the nineteenth century who expounded on this view were called liberals. In Continental Europe they still are. In the pages that follow, I will occasionally use the phrase *classical liberal* to remind readers of this tradition. But words mean what people think they mean, and in the United States the unmodified term *liberal* now refers to the politics of an expansive government and the welfare state.

The contemporary alternative is *libertarian.* The problem here is that many of the leading thinkers of the libertarian movement—Libertarians with a capital *l,* if you will—present a logic of individual liberty that is purer and more uncompromising than the one you will find here. The similarities are great, but I am only a lower-case libertarian.

I am too fond of tradition and the nonrational aspects of the human spirit to be otherwise. I am also conscious, however, that libertarians of the stricter school, fighting a lonely battle for many years, have established equity in the word. Many will understandably be annoyed at my applying the label to views that owe so much to another lowercase libertarian, Adam Smith, as well as to conservative hero, Edmund Burke.

But it is also true that I have considerable company. A growing wing of libertarian thought has been working to reconcile the imperatives of human freedom with the indispensable roles that tradition and the classical virtues play in civic life. In an etymologically perfect world these people would still be called liberals, but they call themselves libertarians without fretting about it. From now on I will, too.

And a Note on Style

Regarding the use of third-person singular pronouns, I apply a rule that I wish would become standard: Unless there is a good reason not to, assign the gender of the principal author. I use *he* throughout.

I

THE FRAMEWORK

*In which are described
limited government's principles, purposes,
and constituent parts.*

Principles

PUBLIC CELEBRATIONS OF FREEDOM used to be at the heart of America's pride in itself. When we bragged about being American (and how we used to brag), it was freedom we talked about, endlessly. We loved our liberty—the God-given, inalienable, constitutionally guaranteed right of every American to live his life as he saw fit, beholden to no one, taking his own chances, pursuing happiness in his own way, doing as he damn well pleased. We celebrated that individualistic, unfettered American in our politics, literature, songs, drama, and, later, in films.

As socialism gained influence in the twentieth century, it became intellectually fashionable to mock freedom, first in Europe and eventually in the United States. What does freedom really amount to, the left asked, in a world of poverty? The equal freedom of rich and poor to sleep under bridges? As the century progressed, the same dismissiveness toward freedom, especially economic freedom, spread from intellectuals into mainstream politics. This thing called freedom, we were told, is what the rich talk about when they don't want to face their responsibilities to the poor.

In the face of such taunts American celebrations of freedom faded. We even stopped talking much about freedom. Listen carefully to today's politicians. You will hear the Democrats talk about "social justice" and "fairness." You will hear the Republicans talk about lower taxes and "getting government off our backs" in minor ways, while leaving it untouched everywhere else. But *freedom?* When did you last hear a leading Republican or Democratic politician argue that preserving individual freedom is government's primary responsibility, even if it prevents government from achieving some other noble goal? That our unparalleled individual freedom sets America above all other countries? The first argument is politically inexpedient. The second is no longer true.

In the pages that follow I ask you to meditate once again on the proposition that freedom, classically understood, is the stuff by which we live satisfying lives. It is as indispensable to happiness as oxygen is to life. Much of it has been taken from us. We must reclaim it.

1

Freedom is first of all our birthright. When all the philosophizing is put aside, what has made me a libertarian is a homely image and the answer to a simple question. The image is of an ordinary human being making an honest living and minding his own business—the kind of person who makes up the vast majority of adults around the world. The question is: What does this person owe the government other than to keep on doing what he is doing?

The operative word in that question is *government.* Our ordinary person owes many things to many people and institutions—to family, friends, community, church, workplace. But an obligation to the government is unique. When the government decides you owe it something, that obligation is encoded in law. If you break a law, a representative of the government can compel you by force, at gunpoint if need be, to do what the law demands. The right to initiate the use of physical force, usually called *the police power*, is what makes government different from all other human institutions.

What should government be permitted to demand of this ordinary person? Very little. Longer and more complicated answers constitute much of the rest of this book. But the short answer gets to the essence of the libertarian position. A person who is making an honest living and minding his own business isn't hurting me. He isn't forcing me to do anything. I as an individual don't have the right to force him to do anything. A hundred of his neighbors acting as a mob don't have that right. The government shouldn't have that right either, except for stringently limited functions, imposed under stringently limited conditions. An adult making an honest living and minding his own business deserves to be left alone to live his life. He deserves to be free.

2

A more elaborated version of this position depends on two beliefs shared by almost everyone: Force is bad, and cooperation is good. These are simple truths we teach as first lessons to our children. They are also profound truths. Taken seriously, they are the principles for living a good life and the principles whereby government makes the living of good lives possible.

A child learns that the use of force is wrong because it's

not right to hurt other people. More deeply considered, the ban on force derives from this principle: *Each person owns himself.* Self-ownership is unalienable, to borrow a word from the Declaration of Independence—a person cannot sell himself, any more than he can sell his rights to life, liberty, and the pursuit of happiness. It is wrong for me to use force against you, because it violates your right to the control of your person. I may try to persuade, harangue, or cajole you. I may appeal to your reason, honor, virtue, or greed. I may obtain your voluntary agreement in a contract. But no more than that. My intentions are irrelevant. I may have the purest motive in the world. I may even have the best idea in the world. But even these give me no right to *make* you do something just because I think it's a good idea. This truth translates into the first libertarian principle of governance: *In a free society individuals may not initiate the use of force against any other individual or group.*

A child learns that cooperation is good because people stay happier that way and more gets done. More deeply considered, cooperation is good because of the principle of voluntary exchange. Formally stated: *A voluntary and informed exchange benefits both parties.* This characteristic of a voluntary and informed exchange makes a free society possible. It is as true of the small exchanges in life as it is of the great ones. You cannot so much as buy a loaf of bread without observing it.

This does not mean that every voluntary transaction works out the way we expected. We may find out too late the wisdom of the adage that cautions us to be careful what we wish for lest we get it. But there is no other basis so benign for making choices and making arrangements with other people. The only alternative to engaging in voluntary and informed exchanges is to engage in involuntary or fraudulent ones. This translates into the second great libertarian principle of governance: Given that a transaction does not involve the use of force or fraud against a third party, *people in a free society may not be impeded from engaging in voluntary and informed transactions.*

Applied to personal behavior, the libertarian ethic is simple but stark: Thou shalt not initiate the use of force. Thou shalt not deceive or defraud. Anyone who observes both these injunctions faithfully has gone a long way toward being an admirable human being as defined by any of the world's great ethical systems.

But the government is different. It has the rightful and exclusive possession of the police power. For what purposes may the government legitimately use it? There are three.

3

The first legitimate use of the police power is to restrain people from injuring one another. Government accomplishes this end through criminal law and tort law.

Criminal law, rightly construed, forbids the basic offenses that involve initiation of the use of force. Civilized societies have condemned these for millennia: assault, murder, rape, and theft in their many variants. Criminal law also rightly forbids fraud. The difference between criminal law in a libertarian society and in the one we now inhabit is that, while a libertarian society would retain only a tiny fraction of the laws we now have, it would take the few remaining laws extremely seriously. For a libertarian society to function, it is essential that people be deprived of the use of force. In practical terms this means that the use of force is met by such certain and discouraging punishment that few people try to initiate the use of force, and almost all who try live to regret it. Enforcement of criminal law requires police, courts, and prisons.

Tort law refers to the enforcement of legal liability for noncriminal harm that one person does to another, whether that harm is done willfully or through negligence. For centuries an imperfect but sensible body of common law captured a very large proportion of what we need to maintain a civilized society: If you cause harm to another person, you must pay for the damage you have done and "make whole" your victim. If I manufacture a hair rinse that causes your hair to fall out, I have to compensate you for your loss. If I cut down a tree that falls over onto the roof of your house, I have to pay for fixing your roof, getting the tree out of your yard, and cleaning up the mess.

Recently judicial reform has contorted such concepts as *negligence* and *liability* into meanings so far removed from common sense—the case of the woman who successfully sued a fast-food chain because she spilled scalding coffee on herself comes to mind—that today's tort law often seems maliciously unfair. Judicial reform has also made litigation so complex, time-consuming, and expensive that many of us would rather put up with almost any harm than resort to the courts. But these are problems of wrong-headed reforms, not of tort law itself nor of courts. The older common law tradition can be a refuge again, restoring tort law as a flexible, all-purpose tool that enables a vast range of human activities to take place without the interference of bureaucrats.

4

The second legitimate use of the police power is to enable people to enter into enforceable voluntary agreements—contracts. The right of contract and the edifice of law that goes with it is what enables us to do business with people we do not know or have no reason to trust. It also enables us to spell out agreements with people we do know and trust, partly so that everyone can be confident precisely what the terms of agreement are, and partly to insure that the agreements will hold across time and changing circumstances.

The right of contract means that a third party—ultimately the government—will guarantee that each party is held to account. Ideally, *held to account* means that both parties will be compelled to live up to the terms of the agreement. If that doesn't work, *held to account* means that the party failing to live up to the terms of the agreement compensates the other party accordingly. To accomplish this end, the government is permitted to use its police power.

5

The third legitimate use of the police power is the most difficult to pin down and the most subject to abuse. It involves that elusive concept, a *public good*.

For the strictest libertarians, there is no such thing as a public good. All taxation is theft, and no cooperative venture should be financed through coercion. The classical liberal tradition from which I write is not so extreme. Government legitimately does certain things—fosters public goods—on behalf of the entire community. Fostering a public good requires that individuals comply with the relevant laws. The government may use its police power to enforce compliance.

In other words, a person can be making an honest living and minding his own business and still have the police put him in jail. Clearly anything that permits such a drastic intrusion on the life of a peaceful, self-supporting citizen had better be an authentic public good. The topic is important enough, and complicated enough, to warrant a chapter of its own.

Public Good

TODAY THE TERM *public good* is used so loosely that it can mean anything someone thinks is good for the public. But the term has a more thoughtful legal and philosophical tradition.

1

One characteristic of a public good is that it cannot be provided selectively. This characteristic is sometimes called *nonexclusivity*. National defense is the classic example: There is no way to provide for a national defense that omits Knoxville or Cleveland while protecting the rest of the country. Some environmental issues involve goods that meet the condition of nonexclusivity. It is impossible, for instance, to segment a city's air into parcels.

Another characteristic of a true public good is that it can be consumed by one person without diminishing its availability to others (sometimes called *jointness of consumption*). Street lighting meets this criterion for a public good. My breathing clean air does not diminish the availability of clean air to others. Usually jointness of consumption has limits, as those who use the public roads during rush hour can attest.

An activity may legitimately be treated as a public good

when individuals are called upon to do things that benefit the whole community. For example, a democracy cannot function without an educated electorate. The cost of providing an educated electorate should be spread over all those who benefit, which means virtually everyone who lives in a democracy. It is not feasible, however, to administer a system in which individual nonparents reimburse individual parents for part of the cost of educating their children. This is a classical liberal argument for treating education as a public good—an argument, I should add, from which many libertarians dissent.

An activity or facility may legitimately be treated as a public good when individuals benefit from some public service for which they cannot easily be charged. Take the case of an urban road grid that was built a long time ago and now serves thousands of people. It is not feasible to charge individual users on a per-use basis. Government operation of local roads and a gasoline tax to pay for them is so much cheaper and more efficient than administering private roads that it is the unquestioned solution.

These cases, when individuals affect others in ways for which, practically speaking, they cannot be charged or recompensed, are often referred to as examples of *externalities*, or *neighborhood effects*.

2

You already see the problem: This business of defining "public goods" is conducted on an extremely slippery slope. In the case of roads, suppose that we are talking about a town in a mountain valley where newcomers want to build houses on the mountainside. There is no classic justification for treating their access roads as a public good. Let them build and maintain the roads themselves. But, say the local merchants, it will be good for the town's economy to have these newcomers, and a good economy is good for the public (and especially good for the merchants); therefore using everyone's taxes to build the new roads serves a public good. It is this kind of glib thinking that drives many libertarians, even those who accept the legitimacy of "public good" as a concept, to reject any deviation from the strictest definition of nonexclusive, jointly consumable public goods. It is hard to argue with their position. Look at what happened to the power of the federal government to "regulate Commerce . . . among the several states" in section 8 of Article I of the Constitution, which over two centuries of jurisprudence has become the blanket rationalization for federal authority over every aspect of economic life.

I have no magic formula for identifying a stopping point on the slippery slope. But here are a few test questions that are helpful in determining whether something is a public good:

Is the good something that cannot be provided by individuals on their own?

Am I asking my neighbor to pay for a government service that he doesn't want?

Am I asking my neighbor to pay for a government service that benefits me, or people whom I favor, more than it benefits him?

In answering the first question, beware of answers that begin, "Well, maybe it *could* be done by individuals on their own, but they won't do it as well or as fast as I think they ought to." In answering the next two questions, beware of answers that begin, "My neighbor doesn't really understand what's good for him."

If there is no magic formula for identifying true public goods, we can at least do much better than we have in recent decades. If everyone applied the classic criteria for defining a public good plus the three questions I just listed to the current inventory of government activities, a huge proportion of them would be so disgracefully out of bounds that they would have no chance of qualifying as public goods.

3

Natural monopolies represent a reason why something not technically a public good may justify government action.

A system of voluntary exchanges works best when many alternative suppliers exist. As the number of potential suppliers is reduced, the potential problems increase. For example, there could in theory be two or three sets of water pipes supplying a city. But the costs of changing from one supplier to another would be high, and the first water company to get its pipes in place could make it extremely difficult for a competing company to gain a foothold. In practice cities end up with one water company. When this situation arises, government intervention in the form of ownership or regulation is a legitimate alternative. Note the word *alternative.* It is not necessarily true, even in a monopoly situation, that a government-owned or government-regulated system will be more efficient or charge lower prices. Government intervention is theoretically legitimate, but the choice of system is to be made on pragmatic grounds. Which system works best?

Once again we are at the top of a slippery slope. A hundred years ago many railroads were natural monopolies. Sometimes the monopolies were abused, and regulations were imposed. Within a matter of decades, as cars, buses, trucks, and then airplanes began to compete, the railroads ceased being natural monopolies. But the regulations remained. Railroads became the sick man of American transportation. Thirty years ago long-distance telephone service was a natural monopoly; today it is not. This progression tends to happen with all sorts of economic activities as technologies change.

Natural monopolies exist, and they can justify government regulation. But the roster of natural monopolies is constantly changing, and it is essential to keep checking to make sure that the justification for government regulation remains.

4

Two additional prerequisites must be met before the government can legitimately try to foster a public good:

The public good in question must enjoy popular support, as determined through the democratic process. Just because something meets the technical criteria for a public good doesn't mean the government has to do it.

Private property shall not be taken for public use without just compensation. That one comes straight from the Fifth Amendment of the Bill of Rights.

5

Reasonable people will disagree about the exact boundary of public goods, even when a rigorous definition of public good limits the range of possibilities. The mechanism for coping with such disagreements is embodied in the principle of subsidiarity. *The legitimate functions of government should be performed at the most local feasible level.* In law enforcement, for example, city and county police take the lead; state police units come into play only when crimes cross local jurisdictions. The FBI was once rightly restricted (in theory, at least) to crimes that cross state lines. In contrast, "the most local feasible level" for almost everything involving national defense is the Pentagon, with National Guard units providing a modest capability for state governments.

Law enforcement and national defense are unambiguously public goods. For government activities that are less clearly so, applying the principle of subsidiarity says, in effect, "Maybe this is a public good; maybe it isn't. But in either case, the federal government won't make a law about it if it can be accomplished by states; states won't make a law about it if it can be accomplished by communities." The political process ineluctably tries to expand the definition of what constitutes a public good. Keeping the definitions as local as possible acts as a brake. When the mistakes become too egregious, people can leave town.

6

In the last two chapters I have offered a simple set of principles: Each person owns himself. A voluntary and informed exchange benefits both parties. The purpose of government is to protect its citizens from the initiation of force by other people and to provide its citizens with an environment in which they can engage in voluntary and informed exchanges. Otherwise government may act only to provide public goods, strictly defined, observing the principle of subsidiarity and compensating individual citizens for costs that fall disproportionately upon them.

The Pursuit of Happiness

THE PRINCIPLES ESTABLISH what the relationship between the individual and the government should be. They do not explain why that relationship is desirable. Even if we grant that individuals have an abstract right to be left alone in the way I have described, how do they benefit? Here the answers of libertarians become more diverse. In one way or another, however, they have to do with our perception of how human beings pursue happiness. Reduced to its barest bones: *Mindful human beings require freedom and personal responsibility to live satisfying lives.* To elaborate:

1

MINDFUL HUMAN BEINGS . . .

The phrase *mindful human beings* refers to nothing more complicated than people who are conscious of living a human life, want to live a good one, and accept their responsibility to try.

This is not a demanding standard. It embraces people with all sorts of physical disabilities, mental impairments, and moral shortcomings, as long as they try to figure out what a "good" life means, try to live according to their understanding, and accept responsibility for the choices they make. The term *mindful* emphasizes that the possession of a reasoning, self-conscious mind is what separates human beings from all other living things.

This point brings us to one of the great philosophical divides separating libertarians from both modern liberals and many conservatives. Libertarians assume that, absent physical coercion, everyone's mind is under his own control.

Much of social policy since the rise of modern liberalism has been based on the opposite assumption—that people are seldom masters of their own decisions. It is perhaps the dominant theme of today's left: People behave as they do for reasons beyond their conscious control. When it comes to thinking about "coercion," the left holds that mental coercion, emotional coercion, and economic coercion are every bit as bad as physical coercion and must equally be prevented by the government. This attitude is exemplified by recent cases in which women have brought charges of rape against men who have used neither force nor the threat of force. Seduction is not seen as qualitatively different from physical coercion. A salesman who uses a high-pressure pitch, an employer who uses abusive language, a store that raises prices on items that have become scarce—all are commonly seen as using nonphysical coercion that requires the intervention of the government. Meanwhile elements of the right argue as passionately that government should regulate what people read or watch. Their logic is usually framed in terms of bad influences rather than of outright coercion, but the assumption that people cannot be trusted to make their own decisions shares much with the mind-set of the left.

Libertarians reject such arguments as they apply to adults of ordinary mental and emotional competence because that position conflates events that are fundamentally unlike. There is no such thing as intellectual or emotional or economic *force*. People may try to deceive me. That is fraud, a criminal offense. People may defame me to third parties or use the threat of force. Those are anciently recognized torts of assault, and I am owed redress. But a high-pressure salesman who is telling me the truth (an important caveat) is not using force against me. As long as I remain physically free from constraint, physically free to pursue options, the choices I make remain my own. When people say instead that they cannot be held responsible for what they think or what choices they make, they are no longer mindful. When we say such things of other people—"They can't help it"—we have stopped thinking of them as mindful.

This does not mean that individuals must have equally strong wills. People need not have especially strong wills if they do not have to contend with force or fraud. Consider how often physical force, the threat of physical force, or fraud underlies what people loosely think of as mental coercion—the high-pressure salesman who fraudulently misrepresents the terms of the deal; the controlling husband who relies on the threat of physical force even if he never actually strikes his wife. When it comes to "economic coercion," a stronger statement is warranted: Its effectiveness almost always depends on fraud, the threatened use of physical force, or the prior use of physical force.

I insert the qualifier *almost always* because a natural monopoly can engage in something close to economic coercion. Other than those rare cases it is difficult to think of a case of authentic economic coercion in a free economy. The stories about evil capitalists forcing their workers to pay ruinously high prices at the company store or their suppliers to sell to them at ruinously low prices always involve the use of goons, or the threat of goons, to shut out competition. People in a libertarian state have recourse against goons as well as against lesser levels of economic malfeasance.

Predators in a libertarian state are forced back upon a paltry set of tools. They must try to do their harm with words, and honest words at that. In a world where there will always be predators, this is as toothless a bunch as you will find. The essence of the libertarian position is the schoolyard chant, "Sticks and stones can break my bones, but words can never hurt me." As children we used it as a talisman against the kinds of hurt that words can indeed cause. As adults we need to remember it as an important truth about what it means to be a mindful human. Physical force is different from words. The elements that go into intellectual and emotional appeals, whether for good ends or bad, are the stuff of social intercourse.

Mindful is not a hard thing to be, is even a hard thing *not* to be. But the question remains: What about people who are not mindful? What about those who say that they are not responsible for their choices in life? Who deny that there is such a thing as living a good life, or any responsibility to try for that end? This book does not apply to them. They do not need freedom and responsibility to live satisfying lives—for that matter, it is hard for me to imagine what the phrase *satisfying life* might mean to them. They are welcome to live out their lives as they please, finding whatever community suits them best. They may not, of course, demand that the rest of us change our lives to accommodate them.

2

MINDFUL HUMAN BEINGS REQUIRE FREEDOM . . .

There is nothing complicated or exotic about the essence of freedom. Freedom is made up of the thousands of choices, large and small, unhindered by government, by which we shape our careers, our families, our communities, our identities. But if freedom is ultimately a simple concept, the classical understanding of it has several aspects that raise distinct issues.

3

The first aspect of freedom is *freedom of association*. Hardly anyone, including the most ardent libertarian, wants to live alone on a mountain top, personally "free" but without anyone to share his life. The need for intimacy with other human beings, for companionship and love, is only a short step beyond our primal human needs for safety, food, and shelter. It is not just that humans are social animals. Our lives are defined largely by the networks of affiliation that we form with other human beings, and it is through the freedom to affiliate—freedom of association—that we build the little platoons through which we live out our lives.

The phrase *little platoons* is Edmund Burke's. He was drawing an analogy with the army: Soldiers die not for king and country, but for the comrades in their platoon. The same is true of the way we live our lives. It is a truth so widely accepted that, like many great truths, it has become a cliché: It makes no difference how much money you make or how famous you get, your real sources of happiness are close to home, in the form of family, friends, and faith.

We must be able to affiliate with, or to shape, little platoons that accord with our beliefs. Part of being a mindful human being is to have a set of beliefs about how the world ought to work and how human beings ought to behave. There is no choice in the matter: It is very difficult—impossible?—to live a satisfying life unless we are able to live according to our beliefs and to see those beliefs validated by others. We achieve this state of affairs by affiliations with people and places. We seek out spouses and neighbors and friends and business associates who share our beliefs.

This does not mean that an Episcopalian necessarily wants to live only with other Episcopalians. People differ in their needs to live among people who are similar. Some of us prefer homogeneous neighborhoods with "people like us"—which can mean other middle-class people, other whites, other blacks, other gays, other Episcopalians. Others of us relish neighborhoods that are filled with all kinds of people behaving in all kinds of ways. To want to live in a heterogeneous, colorful neighborhood is in itself part of the constellation of beliefs that defines a person, and the appropriate neighborhood must be filled with others who share that aspect of his beliefs; otherwise the neighborhood won't work.

In still other cases, beliefs involve elements that can be lived out only when we associate with like-minded people. If I am a businessman who wants to do business with a handshake, I have to associate with other businessmen who think the same way. If I am a parent who thinks that teenagers' parties should be chaperoned, it is important that I live among other parents who agree with that view.

We hardly ever live within little platoons that work exactly the way we prefer. There are always trade-offs. Over the course of our lives we may change our preferences several times. But at any given time we keep tending toward the situation that we desire—within the limits of our freedom to do so.

We achieve few of these affiliations with seals and papers. The process of building our little platoons is haphazard, formless, and endless. It is partly rational, partly instinctive, partly happenstance. It occasionally occurs in big steps, but mostly it takes place in tiny, incremental ones. Freedom of association is central to the process.

4

The next aspect of freedom is *economic freedom,* which embraces the right to engage in voluntary and informed exchanges of goods and services without restriction. Without economic freedom, freedom of any other kind cannot exist except in a pinched and lifeless way. Thinking otherwise has been one of the most pernicious mistakes of the left.

Economic freedom is crucial, first, because you cannot restrict economic freedom without also restricting other expressions of freedom. It cannot be otherwise, for too many of the apparently noneconomic choices we make from day to day are ultimately underwritten by economic transactions. The more economic freedom is lost, the more widely and deeply every other form of freedom is affected. Consider freedom of speech. In a true socialist economy I could still retain the right to stand on a street corner and shout into the wind, but the means I might use to make my speech politically effective—newspapers, radio stations, television stations—are under the control of the government. Over time, political and social freedom invariably correspond to the degree of economic freedom that people have retained.

Economic freedom is important also because it naturally restricts the power of the government. Once it is granted that individuals may transact business without governmental interference, the number of things that government can do plummets.

Apart from these considerations, economic freedom is indispensable because it makes a free society workable. The very word *society* implies order. Economic freedom produces that order. Adam Smith was the first to describe the process, which has since become identified with his phrase *invisible hand*. In the twentieth century the economists of the Austrian school advanced our understanding of the process. Their phrase for it is *spontaneous order*. The mechanisms for producing spontaneous order are economic freedom and its by-product, one of civilization's great inventions: prices determined by supply and demand. Prices yield three benefits with broad social ramifications: knowledge, self-discipline, and equality under the law.

Freely determined prices help insure that voluntary exchanges are also informed ones. In a free market a Honda and a Yugo carry different price tags, and the difference reliably tells you a lot about their relative quality even if you are ignorant of automobile technology. The more the government interferes with prices, the less the consumer knows, and the harder it is for everyone to make informed, voluntary exchanges.

Freely determined prices give individuals a way of calibrating their own needs and priorities. All of us constantly incorporate the role of monetary cost into the large decisions of our lives. It is a constraint that most parents, even those rich enough to give their children a lifetime of financial independence, deliberately impose on their children until they have become adults. It is hard to raise children to steer their lives wisely if they have never known the steadying constraint of the question, "Can I afford it?" Trying to decide whether something is worth it to us in cash is one of the most innocuous and least deforming ways of thinking about the way we are living our lives. Whenever the government abridges economic freedom, those calculations become not only tortuous but deformed. The behavior of people in a city with rent control is an obvious example, as otherwise honest tenants pay bribes to get a rent-controlled apartment or surreptitiously sublet to make a profit on the rent-controlled apartment for which they hold the lease, while otherwise honest landlords scheme to force tenants out of their apartments.

Freely determined prices encourage equal treatment of people regardless of race, ethnicity, religion, or social status. A free price system is a great leveler. Where the economy is not free, you will find a version of the class system that prevailed in aristocratic countries and communist countries alike: Access to certain goods was based not on whether you could pay their monetary price, but on your status. If you were a duke, the law permitted you to confiscate and control in ways that were closed to commoners. If you were a member of the Soviet *nomenklatura,* you were allowed to shop in the special stores with the good cuts of meat and the designer jeans. In a market with freely set prices, all you need is the money. Maybe that doesn't make much difference if we're talking about buying a yacht, but it makes a lot of difference when we're talking about buying jeans. No groveling, no bloodlines, no connections are necessary. In a world where just about everything has a price, the monetary price determined by free exchanges is the least arbitrary, most accommodating to individual tastes, and least subject to abuse.

5

I have been discussing the virtues of economic freedom without mentioning the point that is now most broadly accepted: The freer a market is, the more abundantly it produces wealth. Thirty years ago free-market economists had to go to great lengths to make their case. Now it is taken for granted, and rightly so. I have not dwelled on it because, to me as to many libertarians, it is a secondary issue. The free market's efficiency is a pleasant bonus. It would be morally superior to socialism even if it were less efficient in producing wealth. Protecting economic freedom would still be the only way to assure that people can live free lives.

6

The next aspect of freedom is *property rights*. Perhaps a better way to put it is that no form of behavioral freedom can exist without a foundation of property rights.

Because property rights are so easily dismissed as something mostly involving rich people and real estate, it is important first to emphasize how pervasive property rights are. Technological innovation and the entertainment industry depend on intellectual property rights in the form of patents and copyrights, for example. But even when it comes to physical property, everyone's daily life depends on property rights. Imagine, for example, a world in which there are no property rights whatever; nobody can say of anything that he owns it. The result would be the law of the jungle. You would have no legal right to refuse to let a stranger come in off the street and walk off with your television, no right to complain to the police if the same stranger takes food from your plate. The legal force behind your right to lock the door of your home against an intruder depends on your property rights in the lock and the door. Nor does this state of affairs change if you rent your home; a rental agreement has meaning only insofar as it conveys property rights, delimited in extent and time, from the owner to the renter.

Property rights are a way of distinguishing between thine and mine. They are the material by which even the humblest person can demarcate the sphere within which he makes the decisions. Without property rights everything else falls apart.

Property rights are essential to a free society in the same way a freely determined price structure is essential. Like prices, property rights induce people in a free society to behave in ways that benefit the community as a whole, despite the absence of laws compelling people to act in such ways. It is among the most elementary of human responses: We take care of things we own. If you want to see mowed lawns, tended gardens, and unbroken windows, go to a neighborhood where everyone owns his own home. If you want to see forests that are being managed in environmentally sound ways, visit privately owned forests.

Self-interest is the economist's explanation for this phenomenon. The home or forest will have more resale value if it is treated well. But something else is at work—something most readers will recognize in their own behavior. Knowing that something is yours makes it your responsibility. Ownership is a way to bring out the best in human beings. Property rights are a basis not only for human freedom but also for careful stewardship.

7

If the government guarantees freedom of association, economic freedom, and property rights, there are not many unprotected kinds of freedom to worry about. Nonetheless, it is worth stating the principle of the last aspect of freedom, *freedom of personal behavior*. A lone adult should be permitted to engage in any activity of his choice in private. This freedom includes whatever he wants to read, watch, say, listen to, eat, drink, inject, or smoke. He may dance, sing, pray, chant, contemplate the stars or howl at the moon, and otherwise occupy himself however he wishes. Groups of adults have the same freedom, with the usual proscriptions against force and fraud.

I have put the discussion of this aspect of freedom last because freedom of personal behavior gets far more attention than it deserves when people argue about libertarianism, as if libertarians were concerned primarily with legalizing drugs or establishing the right to publish pornography. Freedom of personal behavior is a central principle of liberty, but in reality few people have the desire or need to test the limits of personal behavior in the course of everyday life. In contrast, all of us not only test limits but run into barriers every day when we try to exercise freedom of association, economic freedom, or property rights.

8

Here are some things that freedom is not:

Freedom of personal behavior is not license. Do people have a right to sunbathe nude on a beach or shout obscenities in a subway car? They may have *permission,* if the owner of the beach or subway car gives it, but nothing in a classical understanding of freedom says that owners must give that permission.

Freedom of association does not compel other people to let you associate with them. They are not obliged to employ you, buy from you, let you teach in their child's school, join their country club, or let you march in their parade.

Freedom does not give you a choice among unlimited options. All actions have a cost. Being *free* to buy caviar is not the same as being *able* to buy caviar. Being free to see a sunset over the ocean is not the same as being on a western coastline on a clear day with good eyesight. Being free to have coffee after dinner does not mean having a nervous system that lets you get to sleep that night. Life limits options. Governments limit freedom.

9

MINDFUL HUMAN BEINGS REQUIRE PERSONAL RESPONSI-
BILITY . . .

Freedom and responsibility are as inseparable as opposite sides of the same coin. If you live in a genuinely free society, you get to shape your own life. You also bear the consequences of your decisions. You are free to live beyond your means, but in that case you had better be prepared for bankruptcy. You are free to put high prices on cheap products, but be prepared to see your customers go elsewhere. You are free to build a home on the Florida coast, but you'd better think about buying hurricane insurance. No law says you have to wear a motorcycle helmet, but neither does anyone have to pay your hospital bills. No law says you can't use drugs, but neither is anyone required to compensate you for your inability to hold a job or to fund a rehabilitation center for you.

The responsibility that goes with living in a free society is often seen as one of its burdens. Responsibility can be harsh, Darwinian, unforgiving of human frailty. If someone has failed to save for his retirement, perhaps for reasons beyond his control, should society let him starve? If parents are incompetent, are we to stand by and let their children suffer for it? These are serious objections, and they deserve the consideration I try to give them elsewhere. But they miss the main point: *Responsibility is not the "price" of freedom but its reward. Responsibility is what keeps our lives from being trivial.*

Think about your own life and whatever its most enduring satisfactions have been—not its amusements or pleasures, nor even its contentments, but its *satisfactions*. They are probably made up of a mixture of pleasure and contentment, but they are something more as well. They are the parts of your life in which you take pride, that make you think you haven't done so badly after all, that define your own sense of what is best in you.

Odds are that these satisfactions involve accomplishments for which you bore responsibility. What filled an event with satisfaction is that *you* did it—not alone, necessarily, but with a substantial amount of responsibility resting on *your* shoulders, with a substantial amount of the good thing being *your* contribution, whether in a moment (sinking the winning basket) or over many years (making a good living). You may be happy that your team won the game if you are a spectator; you may have a good living from a trust fund. But the word *satisfaction* does not apply.

I will unpack this thought a little more, because it has large implications for what government should do. First, there is a difference between theoretical responsibility and personal responsibility. Theoretical responsibility produces theoretical satisfactions. Theoretical responsibility is what happens when I give money to some cause that does good things for people I will never see. Theoretical responsibility is what the politicians are talking about when they tell us that we should think of the nation as a family. The problem with theoretical responsibility is that it doesn't fit the way human beings really feel. It does no good to say that I "should" be as concerned about the deaths from an earthquake in China as I am about the death of a friend. I cannot. "Should" I think of the nation as one big family? The idea is ridiculously out of touch with what *family* means. To think that way would be, literally, inhuman.

By contrast, personal responsibility is what happens when I act in the world immediately around me and when the things I do have an effect on people I know. Taking personal responsibility is a quintessentially human act, and its satisfactions are grounded in quintessentially human emotions. It is only when I take personal responsibility that I can reap satisfactions that will endure.

Two other elements affect how deep and lasting satisfactions are: the degree of effort we put into something and the importance of the function it serves. The importance of effort is so self-evident that it is part of the language— "Nothing worth having comes easily" or "You get out of it what you put into it," or, more recently, "No pain, no gain."

But the importance of function is equally great. If I practice hard as a schoolboy and make the basketball team, my accomplishment soon becomes a fond memory. If I work hard at my vocation as an adult and become very good at what I do, my accomplishment defines an important part of who I am.

Putting these pieces together, I am restating a principle drawn from Aristotle. Satisfaction in human life consists of exercising our abilities and thereby realizing our potential. The more complex and demanding the exercise of our realized capacities, and the more important the function our effort serves, the greater the satisfaction. The rest is amusement.

The truth of the principle accounts for the towering achievements of human civilization. Great art, literature, science, industry, and statesmanship are the products of individuals who exercised their capacities at the highest levels of complexity. But it is a mistake to think of the principle as applying only to a gifted few; it applies to *human* satisfaction. Millions of people find satisfaction every day in doing something well by their own standards. Only a handful of them are doing something as well as it can be done by anybody. But we all have an internal set of calipers for measuring how we perform against how well we are capable of performing, and to approach our personal potential is satisfying—not because anyone tries to bolster our self-esteem with praise but because the observer within us knows what we have accomplished.

Opportunities to exercise our realized capacities depend on freedom. Actually to *do* the thing itself requires taking personal responsibility. To take personal responsibility is to infuse freedom with life.

10

So far I have been concentrating on satisfactions from personal achievement. The satisfactions of social life operate the same way.

Family is the primary unit of social life. For many it is the primary source of satisfactions as well, but nothing guarantees this. To the extent that a household consists of people whose lives are lived primarily apart, there are few satisfactions to be had from family. There is nothing magically satisfying even about having children. If I am the father of a child whom I abandon at birth, I may be pleased if the child turns out well despite my absence, but that happy outcome can give me no meaningful satisfaction. If I pay all the bills for my children's upbringing and delegate the work wisely to good nannies, teachers, physicians, and housekeepers but otherwise have no contact with the children, I now bear theoretical responsibility for how things turn out, and perhaps I can take some pallid satisfaction in my role. But that level of satisfaction is trivial compared to that of the parent who has stayed up all night with the croupy infant, overseen the homework, imparted the discipline, dried the tears, and shared the daily discoveries of growing up. If you want the profound satisfaction that can come from raising children, you have to pay the price.

Friends and neighborhood are the next level at which social life occurs. To the extent that your friends are pleasant people whose company you enjoy occasionally, friends are amusements. To the extent that your neighborhood is where you sleep and nothing else, it is an accessory to your life, like the make of car you drive. Function, effort, and responsibility once again make the difference. To the extent that your friends are engaged with you in the stuff of life—birth and death, sickness and health, richer and poorer, marriage and divorce, misfortune and good fortune, loneliness and fellowship—they can be central to the meaning of your life and to your satisfactions.

11

What are the benefits of freedom? They are embedded in the very meaning of being human. To be human is to be mindful: conscious of living a life and trying to live a good one. Freedom is the raw material for the choices that make up a life—the myriad choices that go into assembling your little platoons, exercising your realized capacities, and demarcating a place for yourself and your loved ones. Responsibility, freedom's obverse, is the indispensable quality that allows us to carry through on our choices and take satisfaction from our accomplishments, whether they be making a living, realizing our gifts, caring for a family, or being a good neighbor.

Why seek limited government? Not just because freedom is our birthright, but because limited government leaves people with the freedom and responsibility they need to mold satisfying lives both as individuals and as members of families and communities. To substitute the phrase that the Founders used so often and so respectfully, limited government enables people to pursue happiness.

An Image of Limited Government

WHAT IS IT, precisely, that libertarians have in mind when they speak of *limited government*? Privatized roads? Privatized police forces? A world in which every personal obligation has to be in the form of a written contract? A society of Ayn Rand characters?

A few do have this kind of world in mind. Libertarian visions of the ideal society are as various as socialist visions, and some of them are extreme. Most are not, however. The country has moved so far from its origins that it is hard for mainstream libertarians to get across how close our politics are to the politics of George Washington, Thomas Jefferson, and James Madison. Their vision of the role of government is essentially the role we see. The size and importance of the official Washington, D.C., they hoped would develop resembles the Washington, D.C., we have in mind. The rights of property and economic freedom that they upheld are the rights we uphold. Limited government is a traditional American concept, not a utopian one.

In the next part of the book I will take up specific topics—civil rights, education, the environment, welfare, and the like—and describe how a restored limited government might play out. Before turning to the specifics, however, an overview may prove useful. Keep in mind that this is an explicitly personal interpretation, retaining elements of government that other libertarians would reject and rejecting a few that others might want to retain.

1

The major changes in a federal government involve the executive branch. The core functions would remain the same. The State Department, the Department of Defense, and the Department of Justice would look very much as they do now, with only some ancillary functions (foreign aid, for example) eliminated. There would still be an Environmental Protection Agency overseeing air and water standards. In my version of limited government Yellowstone Park would still be open and the lights would still be lit on the Washington Monument.

One federal function, education, would become much larger in dollar terms, because a $3,000 unrestricted tuition voucher would be provided annually for each child attending elementary and secondary school—an expenditure of about $150 billion a year. The rest of the federal government would become much smaller.

2

Many aspects of government are not lodged in any one operational function but are widely diffused. Here are some changes that would transform the overall role of the federal government in daily life:

REGULATIONS OF PRODUCTS AND SERVICES

Remaining regulations: None.

Replacement: Manufacturers are liable for harms caused by defective products in normal use. Providers of services are liable for harms caused when the provider's practice is not in accordance with ordinary professional standards.

REGULATION OF TERMS OF EMPLOYMENT
(hours, wages, duties, hiring and firing)
Remaining elements: None.
Replacement: Strict protection against force and fraud by employers in presenting and administering the terms of employment.

REGULATION OF WORKPLACES
Remaining safety regulations: None.
Replacement: Employers are liable for injuries caused by defective equipment in normal use or by work practices not in accordance with ordinary standards. Other on-the-job injuries are compensated through the existing system of workers' compensation funds.

REGULATION OF BUSINESS ACQUISITIONS AND
MERGERS
Remaining elements: Regulation of natural monopolies.
Eliminated: Everything else.

BUSINESS OR AGRICULTURAL SUBSIDIES, EXEMPTIONS,
AND OTHER PRIVILEGES
Remaining elements: None.
Replacement: None.

CIVIL RIGHTS
Remaining regulations: None.
Replacement: A constitutional amendment to the effect that (1) no government at any level shall pass any law that requires discrimination by ethnicity, race, religion, or creed; and (2) no government at any level shall pass any law limiting freedom of association for private individuals and associations.

3

Many specific programs and functions would either disappear or become unrecognizably minor:

HOUSING AND URBAN DEVELOPMENT
Remaining elements: None.
Replacement: None.

TRAINING AND EMPLOYMENT
Remaining elements: None.
Replacement: None.

ENERGY
Remaining elements: None.
Replacement: None.

AGRICULTURE
Remaining elements: None.
Replacement: None.

VETERANS BENEFITS AND SERVICES
Remaining elements: Medical benefits for veterans who incurred their disabilities as a direct consequence of service in the armed forces; death benefits for families of veterans who die from service-caused injuries.
Eliminated: Everything else.

GENERAL SCIENCE, SPACE, TECHNOLOGY, AND THE ARTS
Remaining elements: Patent and copyright law.
Eliminated: Everything else.

TRANSPORTATION
Remaining elements: Maintenance of the interstate highway system.

Eliminated. Everything else.

COMMERCE
Remaining elements: Restrictions on the export of military technology.
Eliminated. Everything else.

COMMUNICATIONS
(such as the Post Office and Federal Communications Commission)
Remaining elements: None.
Replacement: Enforcement of property rights in communications channels.

SOCIAL SECURITY
Remaining elements: None.
Replacement: None.

MEDICAID AND MEDICARE
Remaining elements: None.
Replacement: None.

INCOME SUPPORTS FOR PEOPLE OF WORKING AGE
(Aid to Families with Dependent Children, food stamps, public housing, Supplemental Security Income, unemployment benefits, and social services)
Remaining elements: None.
Replacement: None.

4

That's the wish list, simplified, with explanations yet to come. How much would this stripped-down version of the federal government cost? In the short term a great deal depends on the costs of transition, lasting a number of years, out of the current Social Security, Medicaid, Medicare, and welfare systems. In figuring costs, the raw total of federal expenditures must also be distinguished from net expenditures at all levels of government. The roughly $150 billion cost of a federal school voucher program would be counterbalanced by reductions in local tax expenditures on public schools, while in other cases the end of federal programs might prompt increases in state or local expenditures on similar functions.

Over the longer term, after the transition is complete, the federal government described here would be about two-fifths of its present size, or a federal government that absorbs about the same percentage of the Gross National Product as it did during Franklin Roosevelt's first two terms.

5

State governments are the appropriate place to administer functions that need uniformity across a fairly large area but not uniformity across the whole country.

In a libertarian society as I interpret it, state governments are generally subject to the same restrictions as the federal government. They exist to protect people from force and fraud and to provide the handful of public goods that meet a rigorous definition of public good. There is a place for a state court system, highway patrol, bureau of criminal investigation, highway department, environmental protection agency, and university system if the state's voters want such things.

With limited exceptions such as these, the current state governmental bureaucracies, which have often reached the level of mini-federal establishments, disappear.

6

Under limited government, the principle of subsidiarity—the legitimate functions of government should be performed at the most local feasible level—implies that most of the government that touches daily life will involve municipal and county government.

It makes sense for local governments to be given greater latitude than is granted to the state and federal government, because the smaller the unit of government, the more closely it approximates a group of people acting consensually. The problem is to decide how much more latitude. More latitude, yes, but not unlimited latitude, because local governments can be as tyrannical and corrupt as any other level of government.

Zoning offers an example of the broader dilemma. Ideally, zoning rules provide a way for collections of people to shape the future of their neighborhood and are based on the consensual agreement of the people already living there. Newcomers buy property aware in advance of the zoning restrictions. The government is being used to do something that people want done, and it is arguably doing it more efficiently than private arrangements would.

Occasionally the practice of zoning comes close to the ideal, but not often. Palms are greased, or perhaps the Planning and Zoning Commission simply thinks it has a bright idea. In either case the zoning regulations are suddenly changed to fit someone's, or some group's, special interests. The property owner loses (or gains, if he's lucky), by an action of a city government that is just as arbitrary and unfair as anything that a federal bureaucracy might do.

Should communities then be permitted to pass zoning

laws? If we are talking about a town of a few thousand people, zoning seems innocuous and perhaps useful. If we are talking about Detroit or San Francisco, "local" loses any real meaning for the individual trying to deal with the political power structure.

The same ambiguity applies to other municipal services. The smaller the municipality, the more likely that the services have consensual support. The larger the municipality, the more likely that they are political arrangements for taking from one set of citizens to benefit another.

Given this situation, many libertarians argue that the limits on local government should be as strict as they are on other levels. My own inclination is to give to city and county governments the latitude that the Constitution originally gave to states. Leave federal and state law silent on the rights of local government except insofar as they must comply with the Fourteenth Amendment's equal protection clause.

This is a pragmatic conclusion, drawing from my earlier discussion of the principle of subsidiarity. The smaller the jurisdiction, the more often laws fall into a gray area between the use of the police power and voluntary consensual activities. Trying to prohibit every law with a tinge of gray seems unnecessarily heavy-handed. And while turning even this much of a blind eye toward local government will lead to abuses, there is a built-in safeguard: It is much easier for the average person to move out of Detroit than it is for him to move out of Michigan, and infinitely easier than to move out of the United States.

To that I would add an additional safeguard: Make it easy for outlying neighborhoods in a city to secede and incorporate as independent municipalities. The more aware city politicians are that their citizens don't have to put up with their policies, the more likely it is that city governments will limit themselves to services supported by a consensus of citizens.

7

The great danger in giving latitude to local government is not the size of the city bureaucracy but illicit use of the police power to enforce social norms. Such abuse can take two forms: directly, through repressive laws, or indirectly, as when the police turn a blind eye to the private use of force. America saw abuse of the police power against blacks for a century after the passage of the Fourteenth Amendment, and it continues to some degree today. Illicit use of the police power has at various times and places been used against religious minorities, homosexuals, and political troublemakers. Domestic violence against women has been ignored by police everywhere until recently.

This history is a reminder that some people will resort to the use of force if that option is open to them, and this includes upstanding citizens doing what they think is right as well as criminals and bigots. A libertarian government must above all other things be one in which the private use of force is apprehended and punished and the illicit use of the police power is prevented in the first place.

This rule applies as emphatically to small towns as it does anywhere else. In a free society one of the few people who should be constantly concerned about a higher authority looking over his shoulder is the local police chief.

HOW WOULD
IT WORK?

*In which it is considered
how the citizenry could manage its personal and
public affairs under limited government.*

The Trendline Test

LIBERTARIANS PROPOSE to do away with large portions of government. It is then our job to demonstrate that society would continue to function; indeed, we need to show that a world of limited government would be a better place in which to live. This demonstration cannot consist of proof, just as enthusiasts of a new government intervention cannot prove that their latest idea will work. Policy reform always means a future that is in some ways different from any past that has ever existed. But one general form of evidence is open to us.

1

Government intervention did not occur everywhere all at once. It proceded in bits and pieces, directed at specific goals. The first step in asking whether we can get rid of government is this standard test: Draw a trendline showing what was happening before and after the intervention of government. Here is an example:

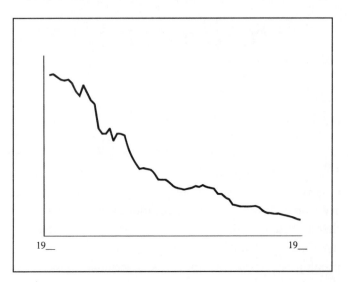

19__   19__

I will tell you what this particular trendline is about presently. The generic form—which can trend up, down, or back and forth—works for almost any kind of indicator of progress.

Poverty? Plot the proportion of Americans below the official poverty line from World War II (scholars have worked out the figures back that far) to the present, then superimpose on that graph the amount of money that government has spent trying to help the poor. Mark the trendline with the dates of major legislation to help the disadvantaged.

Education? Plot test scores or any other measure of educational achievement from the 1960s to the present. Superimpose the amount of money the federal government spent on whatever level of education interests you. Mark the trendline with points showing the landmark court decisions and legislation affecting education.

Health? Plot life expectancy, infant deaths, mortality

rates for different kinds of diseases over time. Superimpose the amount of money the federal government has spent on the improvement of health in that particular area. Mark the trendline with points showing when the Food and Drug Administration (FDA) was established and when Medicaid and Medicare passed.

Safety? Plot injury rates or fatality rates for an industry. Mark the trendline with the establishment of OSHA and major events in the regulation of that industry.

Income? Plot wage rates for specific jobs. Mark the trendline with the passage of the minimum wage act, with labor union legislation, and with the landmark expansions in regulation of business.

Perhaps you are not interested in improvements for the population as a whole but in improvements for the disadvantaged—blacks, for example. Go back then and draw separate trendlines for blacks and whites. Draw separate trendlines for men and women.

The list could go on: unemployment, labor force participation, employment in white-collar jobs, crime, illegitimacy, welfare dependency—any indicator for which longitudinal data exist before and after government got involved.

2

Suppose you have compiled several dozen such trendlines. Here is what you will find:

In a few cases improvement immediately follows the government intervention. Those will be the cases that you have probably already heard about, because they are the ones that have been publicized. To my knowledge the best examples involve the environment, showing, for example, that reductions in some emissions (but only some) steepened after federal emissions standards were set. In other policy areas there are occasional successes—college enrollment of blacks began a sharp increase in 1967, for example. Much more commonly, however, trendlines show a persistent tendency to shift in the "wrong" direction after the government intervenes. Two generalizations may be made for different categories of indicators.

Among trendlines involving social indicators—crime, the family, community, education, welfare—deterioration has been the rule and improvement is the exception. Among trendlines involving safety and health by far the most common result is . . . nothing. Whatever was happening before the government got involved continued to happen after the government got involved. Often a secular trend toward improvement continues. Sometimes the trendline looks like a random walk, bouncing around erratically, and government intervention bears no visible relationship to anything.

3

There is growing acceptance that the reforms of the 1960s largely failed, and many readers will not find it surprising that the trendline test shows that things generally got worse rather than better. But the trendline test may be extended to many of the most sacred of the achievements claimed for government programs, the ones still widely accepted as examples of programs that worked.

Didn't the New Deal end the Great Depression? Unemployment when FDR was elected in 1932 stood at 23 percent. It was as high as 19 percent as late as 1938, and still over 14 percent—still a "depression" by the popular understanding of the word—when Pearl Harbor was bombed. No prior recovery from high unemployment had taken nearly as long, nor had any other required a war to come to the rescue.

Didn't the War on Poverty at least reduce poverty? Using retrospective calculations of poverty, the trendline shows a regular drop in poverty from World War II through the 1960s, with the Johnson years accounting for their fair share, no more. Counting by decades, the steepest drop in poverty occurred during the 1950s, not the 1960s.

Didn't affirmative action at least open up professional jobs for blacks? Blacks were increasing their representation in the professions before aggressive affirmative action began in the late 1960s and early 1970s. The steepest slope in the trendline occurs in the early 1960s, before even the original Civil Rights Act of 1964. More broadly, employment of blacks in white-collar and skilled blue-collar jobs was rising at the same rate before and after the Equal Employment Opportunity Commission went into action. The single exception is clerical jobs, where a surge in government hiring drove up the numbers.

Didn't Medicaid and Medicare improve medical care? If you draw a trendline for life expectancy from 1900 to 1993, you will find that life expectancy was increasing throughout the century; after 1965 the rising trendline becomes flatter, not steeper. If you then hypothesize that the real effects were concentrated among poor people, you may draw separate trendlines for whites (disproportionately not poor) and blacks (disproportionately poor). Same result. If you then hypothesize that black life expectancy has been artificially depressed by the black male homicide rate, compute it for black women. Same result. Suppose you then hypothesize that the real measure of improvement is the *relative* black and white life expectancy. You will find that black life expectancy, only 69 percent of white life expectancy at the beginning of the century, first hit 90 percent in 1955—90.4 percent, to be precise. It never got higher than 92.4 percent thereafter. In 1993, the most recent year for which data are available, it stood at 90.7 percent—three-tenths of one percentage point higher than it was in Eisenhower's first term.

4

The bibliographic chapter at the end of the book directs you to sources that allow you to examine as many trendlines as you wish. For now let me conclude this illustration by applying the trendline test to the one case in which everyone knows that a government law absolutely, without question, saved thousands of lives: the imposition of the 55-mph speed limit in 1974. Go back to the unlabeled trendline that opens the chapter. It represents highway fatalities per 100 million vehicle miles traveled. Could you mark 1974 on the horizontal axis?

Unlikely. Below is the same trendline with the blanks filled in. The trendline begins in 1925, the first year for which data are available, and ends in 1993. The vertical line marks the year 1974, when the 55-mph speed limit passed.

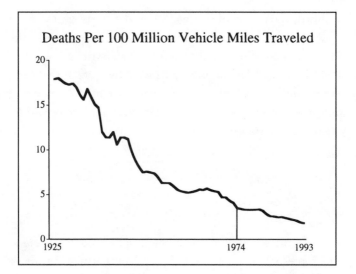

Deaths Per 100 Million Vehicle Miles Traveled

It is a picture somewhat at odds with the rhetoric you may have read about the safety value of the 55-mph speed limit. The period of the greatest change had nothing to do with government regulation. The steepest downward slope occurred in the period 1934–1949, an era when regulation of automobile safety features was nil and highway speed limits, where they existed at all, were high. The only thing that government did was build better highways as traffic increased. Meanwhile manufacturers were building safer cars—not because the government said they must but because greater safety generally goes hand in hand with improved technology in any product, whether cars or industrial machinery or toasters.

By 1974 no change in automobiles, roads, or speed limits was going to make a huge difference—another common phenomenon, whereby the first 90 percent of a problem is much easier to solve than the last ten percent. As it happened, the passage of the 55-mph speed limit made no visible difference at all. It was followed by a six-year plateau in deaths. Even more embarrassing to the supporters of the 55-mph speed limit, the trendline ends with six years of small but steady reductions in the highway fatality rate—beginning in 1987, the year Congress permitted states to *raise* the speed limit to 65 miles an hour on nonurban interstate highways.

5

As I found when I wrote a book called *Losing Ground,* which presents many such graphs, advocates of government intervention hate the trendline test. I can hear their voices now: You can't judge the impact of something with a trendline! It's simplistic! Use life expectancy as a measure of success for Medicaid and Medicare? Outrageous!

For certain kinds of questions the trendline test is indeed simplistic. To understand many phenomena, it is essential to take several factors into account—the kind of thing that complex statistical analysis can do. Logic suggests, for example, that the 55-mph speed limit might very well produce *some* savings in lives, and I have read multivariate analyses purporting to demonstrate that it did. But statistical analyses that take many variables into account seldom make a dramatic difference in our estimates of aggregate impact. In the case of the 55-mph speed limit, the pre-1974 reductions in fatalities are too large to make the post-1974 trendline reductions look impressive, no matter how much tweaking you do.

Even after a complex analysis finds an effect, a problem remains: Statistical analysis of sociological and policy problems is a young discipline, and social scientists are still working out the kinks. The same methodology that seems rigorous when it shows a positive effect of the 55-mph speed limit from 1974 to 1986 suddenly looks much less solid when applied to the reductions in highway deaths from 1987 to 1993, when speed limits were going up—it becomes too easy to use exactly the same methodology to "prove" that higher speed limits save lives. The hard sciences can demand replicability of results as a test of validity; the soft sciences have yet to figure out adequate substitutes.

Often sophisticated analysis only makes the role of government programs look worse. For example, in the post-1965 era the government spent billions of dollars not just on Medicaid and Medicare but also on a multitude of other programs, from job training to welfare, that were intended to benefit poor people in general and blacks in particular. Insofar as they worked, they should have produced a narrowing of the gap in life expectancy independently of Medicaid and Medicare. That the raw gap did not narrow is made more ominous, not less, by detailed analysis.

For purposes of assessing large main effects in public policy, the trendline test is simple, yes; simplistic, no. If Medicaid and Medicare resulted in a significant improvement in medical care for poor people, it should show up in a measure such as life expectancy of populations that are disproportionately poor. The only thing "wrong" with the measure is that it forces policy makers to confront authentic outcomes instead of measuring how hard they are trying. Life expectancy doesn't ask whether poor people saw doctors more often or got more prescriptions. It asks whether their health improved.

In other words, the trendline test asks the question that the public should rightly ask. When the government engages in expensive intrusions on our lives, it does not say,

"Give us 20 billion dollars and a chunk of your freedom for program *X*, and we will demonstrate that the impact of program *X* is greater than zero at the .05 level of statistical significance." The government says "Give us 20 billion dollars and a chunk of your freedom for program *X*, and we will make a large, obvious improvement in American life." That's what politicians promise. That's what they should have to deliver. The trendline test reveals whether they have done so.

For purposes of this book the trendline test offers an answer to the common question, "But how could we get along without program *X*?" How could we get along without welfare, for example, or the FDA, or antidiscrimination laws, or the Department of Education? In the following chapters I will give answers to specific instances. Often, my answer is that we will get along much better when the government has been pushed aside. But the generic answer is this: *Usually there is nothing to get along without.* It is not that government intervention hasn't done *as much* good as people think, but that it has not made *any* perceptible change in the outcomes of life that matter. It is said that roosters think the sun rises because they crow. Politicians are much the same.

Choosing to Do It Ourselves

TWO LARGE REASONS explain why trendlines are so seldom moved in the right direction by government intervention, and both of them are important in understanding why we can return government to its properly limited role. The following will serve as a brief introduction to themes to be elaborated throughout this part of the book.

1

Ineffectuality. The first reason is the simplest: most government interventions are ineffectual. The government huffs and puffs and spends a lot of money, but not much happens, because so much in a modern society has the inertia of a ponderous freight train, running on rails that government cannot shift and moving with such momentum that an outside force such as government cannot speed it up or slow it down more than fractionally.

2

Displacement. Displacement is a more interesting phenomenon than ineffectuality. When a problem develops, civil society begins to develop ways of dealing with it. In the midst of that evolution a voting majority of some legislature says, "Government can do it better," and government intervenes. The government displaces the civil response that would have continued to evolve and expand if the government had done nothing.

The trendline is not immediately, visibly affected by the government intervention because, in reality, there is not much initial change in the net societal activity directed at the problem. Only later, as the government way diverges from the path that private evolution would have taken, does the world of the government diverge markedly from the might-have-been world.

Displacement also explains why government is so likely to make things worse rather than better. Government does not know how to build civil institutions (try to find survivors among the hundreds of community organizations that the federal government started during the War on Poverty). But displacement means that the government is thoroughly capable of stripping civil institutions of functions and effectiveness. One example is found in the extensive social-insurance functions served by fraternal and craft organizations. They virtually disappeared with the advent of Social Security. Another example lies in the web of parental pressures and social stigma that kept illegitimacy rare, combined with the private charitable and adoption services that coped with the residual problem. Intricate, informal, but effective, this civil system could not withstand the proliferation of welfare benefits for single mothers. Government displaces but cannot replace.

3

A return to limited government should not be confused with ending communal efforts to solve social problems. In a free society a genuine need produces a response. If government is not seen as a legitimate source of intervention, individuals and associations will respond. If instead government is permitted to respond, government will seize the opportunity, expand upon it, and eventually take over altogether.

To choose limited government is to choose once again to do things ourselves.

Removing Government from Economic Life

THE PROPOSAL: *As regards products and services, ratify a constitutional amendment to the effect that (1) Congress shall provide for the enforcement of laws against fraud and deceptive practice and shall provide for efficient administration of civil tort law, and (2) Congress shall not otherwise abridge the right of persons and businesses to provide services or to manufacture and sell products.*

In the conduct of business, Congress shall make no law regarding the design, organization, or conduct of the workplace, and shall make no law regarding the terms of employment of workers except for strict protections against the use of force and fraud in presenting and administering the terms of employment.

In this initial description of how limited government might work, I take a more leisurely approach than in the chapters that follow. The proposal just offered involves a central libertarian position: Throw out all regulation of business. (Here simplified, ignoring exceptions involving natural monopolies and pollution that I discuss elsewhere.) The proposal is also sure to evoke a common response to libertarian positions: It strikes many nonlibertarians as absurd. How can anyone realistically think that we can get along without government regulation? The thesis of this chapter is that getting rid of regulation is not nearly as radical a measure as people usually assume and that it is entirely practicable. To work through the argument, I propose a thought experiment.

1

We already know that America can work without regulation of products. *It did work.* To get rid of government regulation of products is not to strike out into some unknown wilderness but, for practical purposes, to return to the early 1960s when regulation of products was still extremely rare. By *worked* I do not mean there were no defective products or accidents, no misleading claims about products or services, but that at any moment in our history the level of such problems compared favorably with the record of any other country's and that the trendlines were moving in the right direction, toward products and services that gave the consumer greater safety and reliability as well as more functionality.

Then came the consumer reform movement at the beginning of a period—1964, and the election of Lyndon Johnson's landslide Congress—when the federal government was mesmerized by what it thought was its ability to do good. Over the next decade a series of legislative acts directed large bureaucracies to write regulations. To this day those bureaucracies have continued to produce volume after volume of regulations, ever more extensive, ever more minutely prescriptive. The open-ended regulatory authority given to the regulatory apparatus produces a built-in momentum. Net regulation has increased since 1964, no matter who has been in the White House or who has controlled Congress.

2

What has regulation bought? Here is the first instance in which it is instructive to examine trendlines. In the case of business regulation of products and services, count up the numbers of injuries and deaths or measures of reliability or efficacy. Then take a representative sample of products and services and draw the trendlines showing what was happening in the years before and after the regulation took effect.

I have already shown the results for the 55-mph speed limit, using deaths per 100 million vehicle miles as the measure. The same applies generally. For some products and services the world was becoming a safer place before the pertinent regulation went into effect and has generally continued to become safer since. For example, in the twenty years before the Occupational Safety and Health Administration (OSHA) was established, on-the-job deaths dropped from 27 to 17 per 100,000 workers; in the twenty years after OSHA was established, it dropped from 17 to 8 per 100,000 workers. Matters didn't get worse after OSHA was established; neither is it easy to make a case that OSHA made much positive difference.

For other products and services the phenomenon known to scholars as *risk homeostasis* applies: give people protection from certain kinds of risks, and some proportion of those people will promptly increase their risk-taking behavior. Result: accident levels that stay level or even increase. This phenomenon was demonstrated most definitively in a controlled study of a taxi fleet in a major German city, where half the taxis were given improved antiskid brakes. The subsequent study period revealed that the brakes worked as advertised—and that the improved taxis had higher accident rates than the unimproved ones.

The net result of the huge federal regulatory push for improved safety and reliability is unknown. The advocates make as much as they can of the reductions they can find after the intervention took place, and surely they are right in some cases (not *everything* can have failed utterly). But what the advocates cannot do, with even the most sophisticated analysis, is assess the displacement effect, which prevents society from developing the alternative mechanisms that would have developed in the absence of government regulation. Meanwhile we can be absolutely certain that we are worse off because of the regulation in several other ways: in the surcharge that regulation imposes on everything we buy, in the limits that regulations put on the things we may buy, in the absence of new products that regulation prevents from being developed.

Above all we are worse off because of the ways in which government at all levels has made regulation an excuse for inspecting and manipulating one of the central parts of people's lives—earning a living. If your personal life were as closely monitored and regulated as the vocational life of millions of Americans, you would rightly call it oppression.

The idea of jettisoning the regulatory system is nonetheless hard for many people to accept. Why not prune out the bad regulations and keep the good ones? One answer is that remarkably few are defensibly "good." The other answer is that you'll never get anywhere that way. If you doubt it, look at the debate in the nation's newspapers and on the television news whenever a bill is introduced that tries to cut away at the edges. Any regulatory reform, no matter how modest, is portrayed as putting consumers at risk so that corporations can reap higher profits. It makes

no difference how far-fetched the claims of peril might be;
to make an allegation has sufficed. Hence the more drastic
solution I propose here: Junk the whole system.

3

As a way of thinking about whether junking the system is
really so unthinkable, join me in imagining that tomorrow
Congress passes a new law and the President signs it. The
new law leaves the current regulatory apparatus and the
current list of regulations untouched. It offers this innovation: Businesses may choose to opt out of the regulatory
system. To make the issue clearer, let us assume that businesses are permitted to opt out of state and local regulations as well.

The only requirement of the law is that any business
choosing to opt out must identify itself, like Hester Prynne
with her scarlet *A*. An unregulated store must post a large
sign reading UNREGULATED where it cannot be missed.
Manufacturers who choose to opt out must stamp the word
UNREGULATED on the package or the shipping container.
UNREGULATED must be prominently visible in every television or print advertisement for an unregulated good or
service. By contrast, businesses that choose to remain
within the regulatory system are free to display equally
prominent signs reading something like, THIS BUSINESS
PROUDLY COMPLIES WITH ALL GOVERNMENT REGULA-
TIONS.

If this law is signed tomorrow, what will begin to happen the day after tomorrow?

There are a few certain outcomes. First, just about every
small business will want to be unregulated. No more forms

to fill out, reports to file, government lawyers to fight. No more OSHA inspectors or endless waits for an agency to process your plea. No more building inspectors, elevator inspectors, or restaurant inspectors. Owners of unregulated small businesses will have to answer to no one but their customers.

I specify *small* businesses, because many large corporations will not be thrilled with the new system. For them regulation is often part of a cozy partnership with government. They can absorb regulatory costs better than small businesses and thereby gain a comparative advantage. They have the lobbying clout to have the regulations tilted their way and to get a tailor-made tax break as a quid pro quo. But many large corporations will nonetheless opt out of the regulatory system once their smaller competitors are no longer hamstrung because they will see the competitive handwriting on the wall.

Namely: Unregulated businesses can offer their customers a much better deal than can their regulated counterparts. Lower prices are one obvious lure—anything from a few percent to more than half off the regulated prices, depending on the product or the service. But lower prices are not the only advantage. Unregulated businesses can also take some of their cost savings and plow them back into the business—offering a more attractive store, better service, or a better product.

If an unregulated business can offer both lower prices and a better product, the contest is over for a wide range of enterprises. Few people will choose to pay an extra dime for a candy bar because they know it is made in a regulated factory, and the same goes for everything from paper towels to computers. Few people are going to choose an overnight delivery service or a dry cleaner on the basis of whether it complies with government regulations. For a few services it is harder to predict what happens. Do many people think that city restaurant inspectors have any meaningful effect on the quality of restaurants? I doubt it, but an attractive feature of the thought experiment is that we do not need to predict. Inspected and uninspected restaurants are both free to seek out their markets.

4

Opting out of the regulatory system does not mean that manufacturers and service providers are off the hook. When it comes to the use of products and services, the simple conditions are these: People need adequate information. They need recourse against others' negligence.

The legal profession has an elaborate vocabulary to describe the old principles of common law that once provided these conditions. I will state five of them in informal language and let the lawyers encode them:

1. The manufacturer of a product or the provider of a service has a legal responsibility to provide clear information about how to use the product or service and to describe the major risks that might be involved.

2. The buyer of a product or service has the responsibility to exercise reasonable care in using the product or service.

3. The manufacturer is liable if a harm occurs because the product was defective in normal use.

4. The service provider is liable if a harm occurs because the provider's practice was not in accordance with ordinary standards of good practice.

5. Contract dominates tort. Individual buyers and sellers are free to enter into written contracts that limit the liability of the provider in whatever ways the two parties specify.

These five principles applied as of about 1960. Only the first (and to some degree the fourth) applies today. A consciously orchestrated set of changes in liability law during the 1960s overturned the others in favor of a philosophy that states the existence of a harm is presumptive evidence that some third party may be made to pay for it. The radical change I propose is to return to a centuries-old tradition of liability, somewhat liberalized.

In reality a very large number of businesses already put themselves on the hook in much more detail than either tort law or regulation requires, offering written guarantees with their products and services, often lavish ones lavishly honored. For the overwhelming majority of goods and services the guarantees and tort law are all the "regulation" that a responsible person needs. Prudent consumers in large numbers will choose the unregulated option because it offers a large, tangible, upside gain and a trivial, low-probability downside risk.

5

Some plausible objections:

FOR SOME PRODUCTS AND SERVICES, IT IS IMPORTANT TO HAVE A THIRD-PARTY ASSURANCE OF QUALITY AND SAFETY.

One example that comes to mind is banks. I like the idea that an independent third party is examining my bank's practices. If I have two banks sitting side by side, one of which has a big UNREGULATED sign on the front and the other one saying THIS BANK PROUDLY COMPLIES WITH ALL GOVERNMENT BANKING REGULATIONS, my first impulse will be to choose the latter.

The unregulated bank cannot change my mind by offering me a somewhat higher rate of interest. When it comes to my money, I attach a high priority to security. Probably many other bank customers feel the same way, and perhaps the story could end here. For a few goods and services it is possible that a substantial number of people will continue to patronize the regulated version, which demonstrates that sometimes government regulation serves a useful function. I will be happy to live in a world where regulated businesses continued to thrive, as long as the unregulated option is open to me.

In fact, however, the story does not end here. Unregulated banks will try to get my business, which means that they must win my trust, and there are any number of ways for them to do so. Moody's and Standard and Poor's, not government agencies, pronounce on bond ratings, and investors around the world trust those ratings. Banks that have opted out of the government regulatory apparatus will adopt some such mechanism. Suppose that Standard and Poor's goes into the bank-rating business, and ask yourself this question: Do you have more confidence in the competence of the accountants at Standard and Poor's or the accountants who work for the federal government?

Perhaps I am still not convinced. I like the idea that the government insures my savings accounts in a regulated bank. If enough people are like me, some unregulated banks begin to use private insurance for their accounts.

They also have to pass along the costs, so now I have a range of choices, from banks that offer markedly high interest rates but little third-party assurance to banks with lower rates but ironclad guarantees. As a consumer I am better off for having these choices.

The same issue applies to other goods and services for which third-party surveillance is desirable—medical care, for example. Even now I am more impressed by the fact that a medical specialist has passed his boards, conducted by a private professional association, than that he has been granted a license to practice by the state where I live. But private oversight groups for medical care have far greater scope than this. Pharmaceutical products and the Food and Drug Administration (FDA) are a case in point.

In our thought experiment the FDA continues to exist, but pharmaceutical companies have the option of slapping an UNREGULATED warning on a drug and putting it on the market without any other permission whatsoever.

I am not going to shift to unregulated medications to save a few pennies. But the FDA is notoriously slow to approve valuable medications, and a wide range of new medications will be developed if drug companies know that they will not have to recoup the huge regulatory costs and delays now imposed on them. So there is a profitable pharmaceutical market to be won by unregulated products. But a very large segment of the market consists of people like me, who continue to be concerned about demonstrated safety of a drug.

To win that market, the industry will need a respected third party to certify its products. In other words, there will be money to be made by setting up a nongovernmental counterpart to the FDA. Such a third party will come into existence, a pharmaceutical analogue to medical examination boards and to underwriters' laboratories, and as jealous

of its professional integrity. Call it the American Drug
Federation (ADF).

For existing drugs the ADF will certify companies as
complying with industry standards of quality control. For
new drugs it will issue various kinds of provisional verdicts.
It will vouch for some as being safe but still of unproved
efficacy. It will say of others that they show evidence of
efficacy but have harmful side effects. It will attach a speci-
fication of its own limited responsibility (as auditing firms
do now), stating that these findings hold true within the
limits of the research it has done, stating what that research
has been.

Will the drug companies be able to buy off the ADF?
Any oversight party, private or governmental, is vulnerable—witness the occasional charges that a Big Six accounting firm or the Federal Accounting Standards Board is in
the pocket of big corporations. The difference between the
ADF and the FDA is that the private oversight firm has a
great deal to lose. If the bond market stops trusting Standard and Poor's bond ratings, Standard and Poor's can lose
everything—be driven out of business. The private agency's
institutional incentives to resist corruption are far greater
than the ones facing government bureaucracies. In other
words, a privately run ADF will do what the FDA *should*
do now: provide an expert third-party assessment of drugs
without trying to be omniscient. As a consumer, having
this source of information is all I need to shift once again
from the regulated to the unregulated option.

Let us take perhaps the toughest of all prospective cases,
federal regulation of airlines and federal operation of the air
traffic control system. It offers an excellent example of a
terrifying possibility (dying in an air crash) and of private
and governmental systems operating side by side.

The first observation is that the air traffic control system is safe not because but in spite of government control. No airplane operated by a major carrier is as technologically antiquated as the government-run air traffic control system. It is inconceivable that a consortium of airlines given permission by the government to set up its own air traffic control system would let its system fall so far behind the state of the art.

The second observation is that the air transportation industry carries on constant, detailed, sophisticated interchange of information—between aircraft manufacturers and carriers, among the airlines themselves, and with the array of satellite technologies and services that support the air transportation industry. The inquisitiveness and the mutual expectations among these parties tend to be more up-to-date and rigorous than those of the government. Among high-tech industries that do business both with government and private industry, a phrase commonly in use is "Good enough for government." It is just as condescending as it sounds.

The third observation is that airline executives dread crashes more intensely than any government bureaucrat. They have much more at stake. A self-regulated airline industry that creates its own code for aircraft maintenance and operations would have fewer regulations and more streamlined procedures, but not looser standards. Under the terms of the thought experiment it might well be that airlines which opt out of federal regulation would suffer some loss of business in the first few years—flying is a high-anxiety activity. But I am predicting that the safety statistics for the unregulated airlines would continue to be just as good as, or better than, those of the regulated airlines. Think of the airline that you are now most nervous about flying. Imagine that it remains within the federal regulatory system, while United, Delta, and American Airlines opt out of the federal system, creating a shared code of standards. Which would you fly?

6

THE BENEFITS OF REGULATION ARE SUBTLE AND LONG-TERM. PEOPLE MIGHT SHORT-SIGHTEDLY CHOOSE THE UNREGULATED OPTION, BUT THEY WILL BE THE LOSERS IN THE LONG RUN.

If the above proposition is true, we will see smart, far-sighted people pay more for regulated products and services while dumb and short-sighted people save a few bucks and choose unregulated ones. If you plan to continue buying regulated products and services, this argument has force. If you know that you will freely, upon mature consideration, choose to patronize unregulated producers, the argument has less force. The most plausible expectation is that intelligence and far-sightedness will be positively correlated with the use of unregulated products rather than otherwise.

7

REGULATION IS INTENDED TO BENEFIT IRRESPONSIBLE PEOPLE. JUST BECAUSE FAR-SIGHTED PEOPLE CHOOSE THE UNREGULATED OPTION DOESN'T MEAN THAT REGULATION IS UNNECESSARY. A RESPONSIBLE PERSON MAY BE ABLE TO USE AN UNREGULATED PRODUCT SAFELY WHEN IRRESPONSIBLE PEOPLE CAN'T.

First answer: To make rules that benefit irresponsible people at the expense of responsible ones is ethically pernicious. Responsibility should be rewarded, not punished.

Second answer: To make rules that protect irresponsible people from the consequences of their behavior is practically disastrous. We should be doing exactly the opposite. The way to reduce irresponsible behavior is to refuse to mask the costs that irresponsible behavior would ordinarily incur.

If these responses seem too harshly unforgiving of the irresponsible, consider a third answer that gets far too little attention: It is remarkably difficult to reduce risks, and it is most difficult when dealing with irresponsible people. Child-proof caps are a case in point. One analysis concludes that a few hundred lives have been saved. Another careful study concludes that the introduction of child-proof caps caused an *increase* in fatal poisonings of children, because people became more careless about leaving such containers within the reach of children. The best bet is that the net change in either direction is so small that it is impossible to pin down.

This is an example of the risk homeostasis I mentioned earlier, and it happens frequently. For example, seat belts can cause accidents because drivers become less cautious. In one sense the trade-off is a good one: The net number of injuries and deaths from auto accidents has gone down because of seat belts. Unfortunately, the net number of injuries among pedestrians and people in other cars—innocent bystanders—increases. It is a nice moral question: Is a regulation justified that saves net lives while protecting the negligent, if it also raises the number of nonnegligent people who are injured or killed?

It is undoubtedly true that irresponsible people will be among those who choose to buy unregulated products. If we were omniscient, we could know who was who and fine-tune policy accordingly. But we are not. People do not have RESPONSIBLE and IRRESPONSIBLE stamped on their foreheads. No personality test, no IQ test reliably enables us to tell who is which. The vast majority of people who choose to buy the unregulated product are doing something that hurts no one and is in their own best interest. They should be free to do so.

8

The examples of the child-proof cap and the seat belt lead to this question: Suppose that a regulation does produce a net good, such as saving some number of children's lives. Is this enough to justify the regulation?

Anyone who answers "Yes" without worrying about costs and benefits is headed down a never-ending road. I can immediately give him another fifteen regulations that will save more lives. His logic requires him to say that all of them are good ideas ("You can't put a price on a child's life"). I can keep piling up the regulations, which involve ever more elaborate monetary costs, behavioral constraints, and police oversight of parental activity.

This is already happening with regulation. The regulatory process is driven by its own logic to try to wipe out the hazards of life. There is no stopping point at which the regulators will say of their own accord, "Yes, some people will die because of hazard X, but it's not worth trying to prevent it."

There is no set of decision rules that everyone can accept, but at least we can frame the question correctly. In thinking about risks and regulation, the question is not what happens to society as a whole but what happens to individuals. Let's go back to the 55-mph speed limit and stipulate that some non-zero number of lives were saved because of the 55-mph speed limit. Was repeal of the speed limit in 1995 therefore a bad idea?

The key to thinking about the answer is this: *Even though the speed limit has been raised, you still have the option of driving at 55 miles per hour yourself. How much safety can you achieve for yourself unilaterally?*

The odds of having a highway accident are small to begin with, the number of accidents caused by excessive speed are only a portion of that number, and the number of cars involved in accidents caused because *someone else* was driving too fast is a small portion of the cars involved in accidents caused by excessive speed. If you unilaterally choose to continue to drive at 55 miles per hour, your increased risk as a result of the raised speed limit is so small that you have to go out several decimal places to find it. You calculate nothing in your life to that level of precision. For practical purposes the net effect on your safety of raising the speed limit can be zero if you unilaterally choose to drive at 55 miles per hour. The difference is that now you may also choose to drive faster, getting where you are going sooner and spending your time—days of time a year, for people who must do a lot of highway driving—doing something more satisfying than sitting in a car. Your choices have been increased, with no necessary downside. Similarly with seat belts and child-proof caps: I am free to obtain the advantages of the regulation by choosing to put seat belts in my car (and using them) or by taking precautions with medicines. The same logic applies to most of the regulations that try to protect us from ourselves.

9

To summarize: In a world where both regulated and unregulated goods are available, everyone may capture the advantages of the regulation, real or imagined, by choosing to buy the regulated product. The self-proclaimed consumer advocates of the world may live just as securely in that world as they do in the one that exists now. They may continue to buy government-regulated products and services. They may also write angry articles, declaim on television, and take out advertisements in newspapers warning the public when they discern a danger. In so doing, they will add to the public's fund of knowledge and thereby perform a valuable service. Here is the difference: In the world of our thought experiment, the "consumer advocates" will not have the right to use the government to force everyone else to share their particular level of risk aversion. They will not have the right to run other people's lives for them.

Why not make the thought experiment real? Politically the answer is simple: Once they are forced to think about it, the proponents of regulation will understand how many of the regulated products and services will disappear from the marketplace. In the real world hardly anyone cares about the things that fascinate the regulators. In the real world people will choose private third-party oversight. If the thought experiment is made real, government regulation of products and services will wither away.

10

I will not go into the same detail regarding regulation of workplaces and the terms of employment. The arguments on safety in the workplace parallel ones already made for products and services—OSHA has brought the nation's workplaces little benefit that is not more efficiently provided by good tort law, but has inflicted great harm on the freedom of people to pursue their vocations. Arguments regarding job discrimination and the end of affirmative action are presented in the following chapter on discrimination and tolerance.

Arguments regarding unions and collective bargaining are more complicated, and skipping them does not mean I dismiss them. Employers, especially large employers, have a huge bargaining advantage over any one employee, and it may be argued that some special protections of collective bargaining are needed. On the other hand, the history of unionization suggests that employers who successfully staved off collective bargaining did so by using force and fraud. Purely economic measures ("If you talk to a union organizer you'll be fired") were seldom strong enough to keep a union out. This leads me to conclude that, as with so many other areas of life, the solution is strict enforcement of the basic laws against force and fraud. A few special protections of collective bargaining might be justified; the problem is how to frame them so that they do not continue to expand—as, historically, they did.

In all cases involving terms of employment and regulation of workplaces, the trendline test applies. Assemble data on changes in wages, working conditions, job tenure, on-the-job injuries, fringe benefits, or any other way of measuring the conditions facing workers and their jobs, plot these over time, and view them against the backdrop of government regulation. It is possible to make the case that government regulation has temporarily distorted some of these outcomes, occasionally for the better and often for the worse. I am sure that for a few outcomes in a few industries it is possible to identify a longer-term positive result. It is much more common to discover that large numbers of jobs in certain industries have disappeared because of government regulation. It is impossible to examine the trendlines as a whole and, after adding up all the pluses and minuses, to conclude that American workers are more prosperous or safer than they would have been if the government had limited itself to making sure that people are free from coercion and interference, free to seek work and to provide work.

Tolerance and Discrimination

THE PROPOSAL: *Eliminate all antidiscrimination laws and replace them with a constitutional amendment to the effect that (1) no government at any level shall pass any law that requires discrimination by ethnicity, race, religion, or creed; and (2) no government at any level shall pass any law limiting freedom of association for private individuals and associations.*

Until the late eighteenth century even the most advanced cultures existed with intolerance so widespread that *tolerance* was hardly a concept. People often did awful things to people who were different: That was the way the world worked. The modern concept of tolerance arose with the advent of free societies. It was in post-Revolutionary America that tolerance for different customs, religions, and ethnicities first became part of a national ethos, most pervasively in the north and west of America, where real freedom was greatest.

1

The relationship between tolerance and freedom is inherent. Intolerance is underwritten by government favoritism and violence. When people are free—meaning that they are also necessarily deprived of the use of force—they find ways to get along.

The view of human nature behind that statement is one that Adam Smith laid out two centuries ago in *The Theory of Moral Sentiments*. It seems more persuasive, not less, as the modern behavioral sciences learn more about what makes human beings tick.

Human beings are social animals, Smith argued. We desire the approval of other people—"approbation," in Smith's language. Human beings are also self-regarding, pursuing their self-interest narrowly defined. In addition, we have instincts that lead us to value our own family's well-being above that of people who are not family, to value our friends' well-being above that of strangers.

Taken together, these qualities leave human beings with compelling motivations to cooperate, to be generous, and to be tolerant if they are deprived of the use of force. Taken together, these same qualities leave human beings capable of every kind of exploitation and atrocity if they are given access to the use of force.

The conclusion follows directly from the nature of force. If I can use force to get what I want, I can live two lives—exploiting other human beings to satisfy my narrowly defined self-interest and finding companionship and approval among the others who are my collaborators in oppressing others.

If I cannot use force, everything I get has to be given voluntarily. To satisfy my material needs, I must persuade other people to trade with me. To satisfy my needs for companionship, I must behave in ways that make others want me to be part of their community. In both cases I must offer something to others that they value at least as much as the thing that they give me.

The link between freedom and tolerance does not depend on people's perfectibility. It does not even require that human beings have a moral sense. It recognizes that, given the opportunity, human beings will exploit each other. Libertarians make this one simple claim, which can be successfully matched against mankind's long empirical record: Deprived of the use of force, human beings tend to cooperate. Literally and figuratively, they live and let live.

2

In a free society freedom of association cannot be abridged. Implicit in this freedom is also the freedom *not* to associate. Individuals and private groups may accept, reject, embrace, ignore, hire for, fire from, lease to, evict from, anyone for any reason. In other words, free people must be free to make judgments about their fellows and to act upon them. This kind of discrimination plays the same role in a flourishing civil society that market prices play in a flourishing economy.

Discrimination has become a synonym for racial bigotry. This perverts an honorable concept. To discriminate is to perceive differences. To perceive differences often means to think that one thing is better than another in some way. Such discrimination is the basis for the thousands of affiliations whereby we gravitate toward things we like and away from things we don't like. We couldn't function without this kind of discrimination.

Horror at racial bigotry has caused us to overlook the social role of true discrimination. Consider the mind-set that gave us antidiscrimination laws in the first place. It is curiously inconsistent. On a few selected issues being judgmental is encouraged. People are free to call other people "racist" or "sexist" on the slightest pretext. But when it comes to anything else, being judgmental is bad. To prefer taste to vulgarity, courtesy to rudeness are said to impose one's own arbitrary values. And yet: To teach your child to hate social injustice is a fine thing, but the lesson will go deeper, and your child will do more good in the world, if you teach your child to be genuinely courteous. It can be hard to know from moment to moment whether one is being socially just. It is much easier to know whether one is being courteous. Conversely it is much easier—not to mention fairer—to judge others' courtesy than their abstract worthiness as human beings. Such simple judgments, *acted upon*, form the balance wheel for social intercourse. Let me give some examples.

3

Employers should discriminate in favor of employees who come to work every day on time, work hard, get along with the other employees, and do not steal from the company. They should hire people who appear to have those qualities, and refuse to hire those who do not.

Store owners and service providers should discriminate on the basis of their experiences with their customers. By all means, give a long-time and reliable customer a special break on credit and prices. It is not merely reasonable but also socially useful for stores to act promptly against customers who are obstreperous or for banks to refuse to lend to someone who has a bad credit record.

Landlords should discriminate in favor of tenants who are likely to pay their rent and not trash the property. To give preference to applicants who show evidence of reliability, sobriety, and honesty will go a long way toward making life more pleasant for the other tenants and for the neighborhood at large.

Schools should discriminate—in whom they admit, their treatment of the students who are there, and what they choose to teach. The ways in which they discriminate should be shaped by the wishes of the students' parents, and differences among schools will be great. But schools should be encouraged to adopt codes of behavior that they enforce as they choose, and these codes usually will mean a set of rules that are openly discriminatory in favor of certain values and punitive toward others.

Churches should discriminate. Whatever the religion or sect may be, it is proper that it hate the sin even if it loves the sinner. In churches and temples that take their religion seriously, "hating the sin" has meant complex forms of discrimination by which good behavior is reinforced and bad behavior is punished.

Above all, parents should discriminate. If the children down the street behave offensively, it is appropriate for a parent to discourage his own children from playing with them and to let his children know why. Parents should express their judgments openly and regularly—not because they will always govern behavior right away (no parent can count on that), but because that is the way that children learn what their parents think is right and wrong.

4

Government is the one entity in society that must be absolutely forbidden to discriminate. Whereas citizens and private institutions have the freedom to follow their tastes and beliefs, the government is permitted neither tastes nor beliefs. Government has only carefully stipulated arenas of action, and within those arenas the only thing that counts is whether a law, stated to the utmost limits of objectivity, has been violated. Whereas it is appropriate for the employer to say to an applicant, "I have a bad feeling about you; I'm not going to hire you," it is not appropriate for a government prosecutor to say, "I have a bad feeling about you; I'm going to throw the book at you." It is the old story: The government can back up its tastes and beliefs with the police power. That is why it cannot be permitted tastes and beliefs. Most emphatically, it cannot be permitted to define one group of people as being privileged over another group of people. It was wrong in the days of Jim Crow laws; it is wrong in the days of affirmative action.

5

Does unabridged freedom of association permit people to engage in racial, ethnic, religious, or other kinds of bigotry? Yes, as long as it is done passively, without the use of force or fraud. This is obviously a defect. In a perfect society, people would not be bigots. Why not outlaw bigotry while leaving other freedoms of association intact?

We don't need theory for the answer. We have history. The Civil Rights Act of 1964 was as innocuous as an antidiscrimination bill could be. It focused on the form of discrimination that is the most offensive: treating two people differently for no other reason than the color of their skin. The bill's language seemed prudent and cautious. Hubert Humphrey, the purest liberal politician of his generation, said of the act that it "does not limit the employer's freedom to hire, fire, promote, or demote *for any reason*—*or for no reason*—so long as his action is not based on race," and promised to eat the printed bill in public if he proved to be wrong. The italics, which are mine, are to draw your attention to the distance we have traveled in the thirty-odd years since the Civil Rights Act of 1964 was passed. Any senator who stood on the floor of the Senate today and argued that an employer has the right to hire, fire, promote, or demote *for any reason or for no reason* except race would be treated as a crackpot of the radical right. To reestablish that state of affairs would mean repealing reams of statutes and jurisprudence.

The bill was apparently a model of reasonableness and good intentions—and it was inevitable that its reach would expand and evolve as it has. Hiring employees is not a mathematical process. Everyone who has ever had the responsibility of choosing among applicants knows how vastly different people with the same paper qualifications can be. But the law cannot look into an employer's heart and know the real reason he hired one applicant instead of another. It can judge only by results, and if too few minorities are hired—or women, or people over fifty, or whatever other protected group is at issue—it is inevitable that additional steps will be taken to promote equal outcomes.

Furthermore, if you permit preferential treatment by groups, the protected group will always be able to complain. At any moment in history a completely fair system for treating individuals will produce different outcomes for different groups, because groups are hardly ever equally represented in the qualities that go into decisions about whom to hire, admit to law school, put in jail, or live next door to. At this particular moment in history a system that is completely fair in its treatment of individuals, judging each case perfectly on its merits, would produce drastically different proportions of men and women hired by police forces, blacks and whites put in jail, or Jews and gentiles admitted to elite law schools. Under the antidiscrimination laws that have developed since 1964, fairness to individuals is no protection from lawsuits.

It comes down to this: You do not have the option of excising the bad kinds of private discrimination and keeping the good ones. They are of a piece.

6

Some people will say, So be it. We will sacrifice true discrimination in order to get rid of bigotry. The evils of racial segregation (or denial of opportunities to women, and the like) were so great that the limits on freedom of association have been worth it.

Here the fact that we passed the laws creates an insurmountable problem for people who disagree. Suppose that in 1880 we had passed laws outlawing discrimination against the Irish. In 1910 the supporters of the bill could have triumphantly pointed out that there were no longer any "No Irish Need Apply" signs and that discrimination against Irish in college admissions had all but vanished. How could I have said convincingly, "But these good things would have happened without the laws"? Suppose that in 1930 we had passed laws barring discrimination against Jews, and in 1960 you confronted me with evidence that anti-Jewish discrimination had dramatically shrunk everywhere during the intervening thirty years. How could I have proved that these improvements would have occurred without the laws? And so it is with the Civil Rights

Act of 1964 and its convoy of subsequent legislation and court decisions. There is no way I can *prove* that they were unnecessary, even though we know that in the first two instances I would, in fact, have been right and the proponents of the antidiscrimination laws would, in fact, have been wrong. But if proof is impossible, there are these things to consider:

7

Go back to the newspaper indexes for the years immediately *preceding* the passage of the Civil Rights Act of 1964, and you will find a steady sequence of stories about hotel chains and restaurants and other service providers renouncing racial favoritism or segregation in their operations. Replay the kinescopes of newscasts and documentaries or read the civil-rights coverage in *Time* and *Newsweek* from the years just before 1964, and you will observe a nation run by whites coming to grips with the injustice of racial prejudice in ways that would have been unthinkable a decade earlier. America did not make progress against racism because Congress passed the Civil Rights Act of 1964; Congress passed the Civil Rights Act of 1964 because the nation was so committed to make progress against racism.

The good effects of the Civil Rights Act of 1964 were bumps on top of a much larger, more powerful, and healthier trend that was occurring in civil society and would have continued if the government had done nothing. The price of those bumps was to give a moral crusade over to the bureaucrats. Many of the social forces that led to cooperation and mutual accommodation dried up. Many of the social forces that led to confrontation and hostility were energized. Many blacks saw themselves as victims with a never-to-be-satisfied list of grievances. Many whites stopped wrestling with their consciences and saw themselves as the victims of reverse discrimination. A sense of working out this difficult problem together, as Americans with common bonds transcending race, was lost.

8

Parallel comments apply to gender. Women's understanding of their role in society changed profoundly in the postwar era, accelerating from the end of the 1950s through the 1960s. Women were not given permission to change their understanding by government antidiscrimination laws; the antidiscrimination laws passed because so many women had already changed their views. Once again, draw the trendlines regarding employment and wages from the 1950s on. Try to figure out on the basis of the trendlines when the laws changed. Women's progress occurred at conspicuously "wrong" times if you are trying to make a case for legal intervention.

What happened to the civil-rights movement happened to the women's movement as well. Once they could use the law to compel, people no longer tried to persuade. What had been an evolutionary working out of a complicated set of problems became an us-versus-them resentful battle presided over by the bureaucrats and their statistical guidelines.

9

A free society is most threatened not by uses of government that are obviously bad, but by uses of government that seem obviously good. Antidiscrimination law has been a leading case in point. Freedom of association is too precious to be sacrificed for any particular social goal—precious as a hallmark of a free person, but precious also as a resource for making a free society work. The good kinds of discrimination must be applauded. The bad kinds of discrimination must once again be made wrong, not illegal.

Permitting Revolutions in Education and Health Care

THE PROPOSALS: *For education: Deregulate education at all levels of government. Replace all existing federal programs with an unrestricted $3,000 school voucher, per annum, per child. For health care: Treat the value of employee medical benefits as taxable income. Deregulate the health care industry at all levels of government. End Medicaid and Medicare.*

The current problems in education and health, seemingly so different, are alike in defying common sense. We should not be worrying about how to keep weapons out of schools or how to ensure that high-school graduates can read. Instead, we should be enjoying a golden age of improvement in education. We should not be worrying about whether an affordable health care system is possible. Instead, routine health care should have been getting steadily cheaper for years, leaving plenty of money to pay for catastrophic health insurance.

We should be seeing in both education and health the same trends that have characterized other products and services that benefit from new technology—more options and more flexibility, with better value for money in some cases and better value for less money in others. The government has systematically protected both education and health care from the revolutions they desperately need.

1

The current movement for educational reform wants to start teaching the three R's again, stop "social" promotions, reinstall meaningful academic standards, and restore civility and discipline in the schools. These are all good things to do. But consider how bizarre it is that such things need to be done. Only the most befogged educational establishment could have led American education into a situation in which a student gets a diploma without being able to read it or a student can bring a gun onto the school grounds without being summarily tossed out on his ear.

But there is another aspect of education that hardly anyone seems to notice: If all we had to worry about was the objective resources (potentially) at educators' command, elementary and secondary education should be improving by leaps and bounds. All around us children are using technology in ways that should be causing educators to rejoice. The great symbol of educational inertia in our time is the child who comes home from school, finishes his homework as perfunctorily as he can get away with, then sits in front of the computer for hours playing Oregon Trail or Math Munchers, absorbed in learning the very kind of knowledge the school wants to impart.

Children also use the computer to play Mortal Kombat and Dark Forces because they are, after all, children. We should not expect them to figure out how to use the new technology to improve education. That's the job of adults. The possibilities now facing adults are so open-ended, so dazzling that the education industry should be in the same state of riotous change as the computer and telecommunications industries. Nothing like that is happening. Public education is the Soviet agriculture of American life.

In holding out the prospect of large improvements in education, I am not trying to evoke any particular futuristic image of the classroom. I assume there will always be a place for the traditional classroom, and certainly one for the gifted teacher. But how much more effectively could they be used? A leapfrogging technology provides so many opportunities that no one can yet describe their specifics. We won't know until the government gives up its regulatory and financial stranglehold on elementary and secondary education.

2

The problem with health care is not with its excellence but with its organization. By the mandate of law supported by intricate regulation, all of American medicine goes through a bottleneck called the physician, converting what should be one of several choices into a requirement.

Routine health care should work something like this: A person gets sick. Some very large proportion of the time the problem he is experiencing is a garden-variety illness with a straightforward, well-established treatment. If so, the patient is given routine treatment. If there is a chance that something more complicated is involved, the patient sees someone who is especially trained to make the more difficult diagnosis. If a more complex or difficult treatment is required, the patient gets the appropriate specialized treatment.

In a large portion of all garden-variety medical complaints—of all health care, in other words—a physician shouldn't be directly involved. Take the case of diagnosis. We patients want a physician because we imagine his highly trained brain, informed by years of experience, sifting through the possibilities, making subtle judgments. Once upon a time that was probably the best option. Today you are likely to be better off with an experienced nurse practitioner armed with a protocol of questions, sophisticated diagnostic software, and specialized human backup for ambiguous calls.

What is true for diagnostic software is true for dozens of other technological innovations in medicine. As medical knowledge and technology advance, we take for granted that some kinds of health care must get more and more expensive, but it shouldn't be that way for routine care. Every expensive new MRI device or heart-lung machine that patients need at moments of medical crisis has many less dramatic counterparts that make routine medical tasks cheaper, less complicated, more foolproof—and that open up ways in which technicians can do jobs that are still reserved by regulatory fiat to physicians. It doesn't require a medical degree, nor should it cost a lot of money, to close the cut on a child's knee or to prescribe the right antibiotic for an ear infection.

As in the case of education, I am not trying to sell any particular reorganization of the medical profession but saying simply that the current system bears little resemblance to the one that would have evolved if the government were not shielding the medical care system from change.

3

The solution for education and health care is the solution that works in producing every other kind of service. Let people shop for what they want and pay for what they get.

Neither is permitted to happen very often under the existing educational and health care systems.

As regards education: If I send my child to the public school, the bulk of the cost is subsidized by taxpayers without children of school age. I also have virtually no control over what I get from that public school. The decisions are out of my hands, and increasingly not even in the hands of the local school district but in Washington. If I send my child to private school, I have to pay for more than I get—I continue to pay taxes to support the public schools as well as the tuition at the private school. I still have very limited choice. The private school system that currently exists is analogous to the private restaurant system that would exist if the government maintained mediocre but free restaurants—a shadow, in size and variety, of the system that would exist in the absence of the government product.

Meanwhile the health care system is a cartel. A nurse practitioner rarely has the option of opening a clinic offering basic medical care. Such clinics are illegal in almost all states. I as a consumer don't have the option of deciding to visit the nurse's clinic the next time I have a sore throat. I *must* go through a physician if I want to get a prescription.

By government decree my choices for health insurance are distorted so that I become complicit in supporting a creaky system. My employer provides medical insurance, but the government says that the cost of the insurance is not treated as taxable income. The medical insurance is therefore worth much more to me than the equivalent salary increase, and I am shielded from incentives to push for change in the nature of my insurance. Almost everyone would prefer that a highly trained, wise, kindly individual treat us for every sore throat, examine every EKG, pore over every symptom with infinite care, and generally devote his life to the well-being of one's own precious body. Why should I press for deregulation of the health industry if my insurance pays for such a person?

As cost pressures rise, employers have incentives to do whatever they can to hold down their insurance costs. The American health system is trying to evolve in the directions I described, as witnessed by the rapid growth of health maintenance organizations and the increased use of nurse practitioners. But as in the case of the existing private-school system, the changes in health care we observe now are trivial compared to the restructuring that would take place if consumers paid for what they got and if the health care industry could provide its services in whatever ways made the most sense. You prefer that a physician take care of every little thing? That would still be an option, with the appropriate price tag attached.

4

Should the government continue to have a role in financing education and health care? The two functions involve very different rationales for a government role.

Education is a public good insofar as an educated electorate is essential for a democracy to function. But that doesn't necessarily mean that public financing is needed. Some extremely high proportion of children would be educated even if the government got out of the education business altogether. As this proportion approaches 100 percent, the public-good justification for financing education goes to zero. Furthermore, there is good reason to think that the proportion would be close to 100 percent. Prior to the introduction of public schools American communities in the North and West (the South under slavery was another story altogether) routinely made provisions for the education of children whose parents couldn't afford tuition at the private schools that comprised the educational system.

But we cannot know precisely what proportion of children would go to school, and the prospect of any children at all without access to education is troubling. Is public money needed to achieve the public good called education? Libertarians disagree among themselves. I take seriously the arguments of those who conclude that government entry into education in the nineteenth century was a mistake, but in the end I side with those who are prepared to accept government funding, though not government control, of education.

My own preference is to end all existing forms of state and federal regulation, substituting a lump sum voucher for all federal and state financing. Parents of every school-age child would be given a chit worth a certain sum of money that they could take to any school they wanted. The key to doing more good than harm needs italics, however: *A voucher must be wholly unrestricted.* Any attempt to impose restrictions on the vouchers (for example, by making them good only at schools accredited by the government) is likely to be disastrous in the long run.

Counties and municipalities would be free to do as they pleased. They could maintain a public-school system to which parents who preferred public schools could bring their vouchers. The locality could augment the school budget with tax dollars, spending as much money per pupil as it wished. Or a locality might decide to forego public schools altogether. It would be up to the local voters.

How big should the voucher be? About $3,000 a year seems right, though the amount is open to discussion. In 1993–1994, well over half (58 percent) of the five million children in private schools, religious and nonreligious combined, went to schools that charged less than $2,500; 86 percent attended schools that charged less than $5,000. But those figures are heavily influenced by subsidized tuition at religious schools. Tuition at nonsectarian private schools (where tuition usually has to cover the full cost of education) averaged $6,631 a year.

In any case, the point of the voucher is not to give parents enough money to send their children to any school in the country but to give parents options. Large numbers of private schools, usually affiliated with churches, would probably charge exactly $3,000. Many of these would employ scholarship systems, funded by the church or parents, that permitted some children to attend for $3,000 even though the cost per pupil were greater than that. Many parents would use the $3,000 as a supplement to their own out-of-pocket costs at more expensive private schools. In communities that maintained a public-school system, parents could take their $3,000 to the public schools.

The dynamics of the voucher system do not depend on the specific figure I have named. If $3,000 turned out to be too low to achieve the desired effects, it could be increased. The nation currently spends about $6,000 a year on each pupil attending the public system, giving considerable room to fine-tune the size of the voucher without increasing total spending on schools.

5

The case for health care as a public good is much shakier than the case for education. There are some exceptions—control of epidemics is an example. Generally, however, using the government to finance health care of individuals is one of those "nice things to do" at the heart of so many government programs.

It is also one of those nice things to do that have produced much less good than people tend to assume. If Medicaid and Medicare were needed, it was because the poor were not getting adequate care (the rich have always gotten the best care available). If Medicaid and Medicare worked, we should observe a pattern in which health outcomes for the poor improved faster than they did for the rich. Instead, the message of the trendlines is that health improved dramatically over the last half century, for everyone, before Medicaid/Medicare and after. Recall the earlier discussion of trends in life expectancy among blacks (disproportionately poor) and whites (disproportionately not poor): Black life expectancy relative to whites was as high in the Eisenhower administration as it is today.

It is easy to prove that health has improved for everyone. But trying to prove that many had better health *because* of Medicaid and Medicare is a much more difficult and ambiguous task. Trying to prove that the current system is better than the one that would have evolved in the absence of government intervention is impossible.

6

But the past is past, and health care today is different from health care in the 1950s. Would the entire population have adequate access to health care in a world of deregulated, unprotected health care?

The first and crucial point is that a free market in health care is going to make routine health care something that people can be expected to pay for, just as they are expected to pay for groceries, the telephone bill, and the rent. Paying for your routine medical expenses is part of being a grown-up.

The main new factor involves catastrophes. Before World War II the number of ways in which you could go broke from medical costs were limited. You got sick, you got the available treatment, and you recovered or you didn't. If you broke your neck, it was unlikely you would become a quadriplegic because you were probably going to die before long. If you had heart disease, you didn't have to worry about the cost of heart surgery because there wasn't any. Today every adult should act on the assumption that sooner or later some expensive medical crisis will arise. Today not to purchase catastrophic health insurance is irresponsible.

The bright side is that catastrophic health insurance can also be cheap. For example, a catastrophic lifetime health insurance policy bought at the age of twenty and guaranteed for life could have low, constant monthly costs—in effect, young people who have low health-care costs would be subsidizing their elder selves.

What about twenty-year-olds who don't think that far ahead? A classical liberal may argue, and some have, that government intervention is legitimate for health, perhaps by making catastrophic health insurance compulsory (in the same way that you have to show proof of insurance before you can get a driver's license) or through schemes such as medical savings accounts. They rightly point out that catastrophic health insurance is one of the rare instances in which government intervention poses a comparatively small risk of unintended consequences because little "moral hazard" is involved—few people court a medical catastrophe just because they are insured.

The main risk of government provision of catastrophic

health insurance is that government would insist on heavy regulation of the insurance and health-care industries. Perhaps a voucher-based system could get around these dangers, but the problems are formidable. On balance I conclude that we would be better off if the government stayed out of the health-care business altogether.

7

What about the people who are left out? Who don't or perhaps cannot buy catastrophic health insurance? Who don't have enough money to pay even for routine medical care?

There used to be a system for dealing with such problems. Before the advent of Medicaid and Medicare it was taken for granted that physicians charged reduced fees to patients who couldn't pay full fee. The patients who could afford to pay the full fee accepted the fact that their fees helped to cover the cost of treating patients who could not pay. The patients who could not afford to pay accepted their obligation to do whatever they could to reciprocate eventually.

Before the advent of Medicaid and Medicare localities built public hospitals and clinics, sometimes privately endowed, often financed with tax dollars. They were usually not the fanciest of facilities, but they provided good care and they didn't turn a person away because he didn't have a Medicaid card.

Before the advent of Medicaid and Medicare, medical practitioners saw their work as a vocation, not as just a job. Thirty years ago, we brought that vocation within the purview of government, and the same thing began to happen to health care that happens to every human interaction when it is bureaucratized: It became more difficult to be generous, more difficult to treat individuals on a case-by-case basis, and easier to rationalize turning them away—"Sorry, but I have to follow the rules." Of all the professions, people in the health-care business have historically had the most explicit ethical charge to see that all are served. They met that obligation as matter of course before the federal government became involved.

The system we used to have did not try to pretend, as the current system shamefully does, that it is feasible for everyone to get the most advanced possible health care. It did not tax working people, including low-income working people, to pay for the health care of affluent elderly people. It relied on social norms and pressures rather than regulations and in so doing fostered our sense of mutual obligation. It produced health care outcomes that improved rapidly for everyone, rich and poor, as national wealth increased and medical technology advanced. A health care system without the federal government worked. It could work again.

Sex, Drugs, and Rock and Roll

THE PROPOSAL: *Federal and state laws regarding alcohol, drugs, prostitution, gambling, and pornography are repealed, except for provisions regarding minors.*

Many free-market conservatives do not call themselves libertarians because they do not want to be associated with proposals such as the above. But the issue needs to be joined: Is it appropriate for the government to put people in jail because of things they do that might be harmful to themselves but that do not coerce or defraud anyone else?

This extremely emotional debate involves two separable issues. One is the question of whether people should be allowed to harm themselves. The other turns on the question of whether families and communities can protect themselves from practices they find obnoxious if they do not have the protection of government.

1

The question of whether people should be allowed to harm themselves is the simpler of the two. *They must.* To think it is right to use force to override another person's preferences "for his own good" is the essence of the totalitarian personality. If you have the right to do that to someone else, then someone else has the right to do it to you. That way lies the rationalization for every conceivable kind of coercion.

The practical reality, familiar to every adult, is that we do not have the capacity to know with any degree of accuracy what is good for another person. It is most anguishingly apparent in bringing up children, where the line between keeping children safe and letting them take a chance so as to learn from experience is a continual source of parental worry and self-doubt.

With our adult friends and relatives the question becomes even more difficult. Some people sincerely think their friends who drink martinis and eat rare steaks are doing themselves harm. They may be right by certain medical criteria. But they are in no position to strike the larger balance that the martini-drinking steak eater must strike for himself. What are the pleasures worth relative to the costs? I think the other fellow is harming himself. He sees it as paying a cost he is willing to pay.

In daily life most people accept the autonomy of their friends and relatives. The sequence that finally leads people to confront an alcoholic with the need for treatment is a classic example. You may lecture your friend when you first think that he is drinking too much, but matters have to get a lot worse before you begin to badger him into a treatment program. And properly so.

All this reflects our common human experience. Where and for what reasons need the government come into the picture? What are the human activities that do not coerce anyone into doing something but are so unequivocally harmful to the actor that the government is justified in banning them?

As long as we restrict the issue to the question of preventing the individual from harming himself, I cannot think of any. Drugs? Crack cocaine is one of the most terrible of drugs. But if a person who smokes crack cocaine doesn't abuse his wife or children while he's high, shows up at work sober, and pays for his habit with money honestly earned, what is the problem that society is trying to solve when it puts him in jail? With regard to this narrow question, the parallels with alcohol seem to me exact: The crimes drunk people commit are punishable; the act of drinking is not.

Other issues of self-harm follow the same track. Prostitution? There are valid reasons to arrest most pimps, because they tend to use force and fraud. There are reasons, involving forbidden uses of public spaces, for arresting prostitutes soliciting on street corners. But it's none of the government's business if a man and woman decide, without interfering with anyone else's freedom, to exchange sex for money. Pornography? I favor laws restricting access to minors. I support enforcing laws against the kinds of force and fraud that accompany some of the production of pornography. That is as far as government may legitimately go. Suicide? You do not need a law against suicide to insure that the average citizen will try to intervene if he sees someone about to jump off a bridge. But not everyone who is prevented from committing suicide is grateful, and making suicide "illegal" seems close to the Platonic ideal of the absurd law.

To me, as to most libertarians, it seems axiomatic that the government has no right to keep an ordinarily competent adult from doing something that others judge harmful to him—so axiomatic that it is hard to enter into a dialogue with people who think otherwise. But the practical policy issues are not simple at all.

2

If drugs, prostitution, and pornography cannot be out-lawed, how can families and communities protect themselves from practices they find obnoxious? The argument against legalization that I find most persuasive goes something like this: *Perhaps it is true that some people use crack cocaine without harming anyone else, but a great many crack cocaine users do harm other people. Prostitution theoretically could be a sale of services like any other, but it usually doesn't work that way. The damage pornography does to the social fabric is a necessary consequence of the apparently private acts of selling and buying it. The libertarian's tidy way of segmenting self-harm from social harm doesn't work.*

The principled libertarian response, put crudely, is: "That's tough. Give in on these issues, and there is no stopping point." But while the principled response is adequate in theory, it ends any conversation with people who think otherwise. Let me enter a purely pragmatic proposition instead: *If your objective is to control the social harms done by drugs, prostitution, pornography, and the like, you are going to be able to do it most easily in one of two societies: a totalitarian state or a genuinely free society. The in-between society in which we now live is the place where vice becomes an unmanageable problem.*

Vices thrive when they are subsidized and protected, and that's what the current system does—through the welfare system for those who have incapacitated themselves, and through pervasive restrictions on freedom of association. Can the proscribed activities be safely legalized if the rest of the libertarian agenda is also enacted? Yes. Individuals and communities will be much better able to protect themselves than they are now. I will use the most controversial item—drugs—to make the general argument.

3

The United States has spent billions of dollars on antidrug efforts, tied up a large proportion of the nation's police and courts, and imprisoned hundreds of thousands of people, thereby proving that no suppression policy short of totalitarianism has much effect on the price and availability of drugs. But the irony is that it wouldn't have made any difference if the War on Drugs had achieved its stated goals through all of this activity. The goals of the War on Drugs, like the goals of most government programs, are more relevant to bureaucrats than to daily life.

So what if the government succeeds in reducing national cocaine use by 20 percent? What most of us want from a drug policy is a world in which *our* children do not get hooked, not one in which there is 20 percent less cocaine in circulation. The proper question of what constitutes "success" regarding the drug problem is that *you* be able to live in a world where *you* and *your* family are as safe from drugs as you want to be. What is the selfish solution that would work for you, whether or not it rids the entire nation of drugs? If you state the goal in this parochial way, some of the answers become relatively simple.

4

Perhaps the thing about drugs that most immediately worries you is that your child is going to a school where there is a known drug problem. Step back from the issue, quit brooding about societal ills and the complex causes of the national drug problem, and think about how absurd it is that the school your child attends has a drug problem. It is not hard for teachers and principals to control schools if they have a free hand to oversee, discipline, suspend, and expel students, 1950s-style. In other words, if you want a world in which your child is not exposed to drugs in schools, don't have the government outlaw drugs; send your child to a school that outlaws drugs.

If I am a parent who is really afraid of drugs, I will choose a school with zero tolerance—expulsion for the first infraction and frequent, unannounced locker checks. If I am moderately afraid, I will choose a school with a slightly more relaxed policy. If I am not afraid at all, I will choose a school where the administration cannot touch my child without due process and a search warrant. Wherever I stand on this spectrum, I know how to send my children to a school that is as drug-free as I wish—if there is a free market in schools. The most effective anti–drugs-in-schools policy? Unrestricted educational vouchers.

I began with the school system because it offers a clear example of the policy revisions I have in mind. But the school example generalizes. Translated into a policy goal for the War on Drugs, it reads like this: *People should be free to live in neighborhoods that are as drug-free as they wish, work in workplaces that are as drug-free as they wish, and send their children to schools that are as drug-free as they wish; and this should be true for poor people as well as rich people, blacks as well as whites, people who live in cities as well as people who live in small towns.*

If you, personally, could live in a neighborhood, work at a job, and send your children to schools where drugs weren't a problem—and if everyone else could too, if they wanted—wouldn't that pretty much give you what you want in the war against drugs? It is easily done. The same principles that work for the school—freedom of association combined with freedom to conduct one's business as one sees fit—apply to the workplace and the neighborhood as well as to schools.

5

Regarding the workplace: Employers should be free to specify whatever drug policy they like as a condition of employment, subject to the collective bargaining agreement where applicable. It is up to a job applicant to decide whether he wants to take a job under those rules. A few employers will impose drug testing so stringent that the employees can't afford to do drugs, on or off the job. Most employers will do what common sense says to do: They will run a workplace in which employees have to show up sober and stay sober during the workday.

Few employers will knowingly hire drug users; virtually all employers will quickly take action when a drug problem is discovered, usually by firing the person involved. This response will result in workplaces where drugs are not a problem, and it will also serve as a powerful incentive for people not to use drugs or to make sure that the habit doesn't become debilitating. The most effective anti-drugs-in-the-workplace policy? Free employers from government regulations over terms of employment.

6

Regarding the neighborhood: Among affluent adults the question is trivial. There is adult drug use in some affluent neighborhoods, but it is not "illegal" except in the most theoretical sense—very few cells in the nation's jails are occupied by affluent drug users. What drug use does exist among the affluent does not contaminate the community nearly as visibly as it does in poor neighborhoods. The children on their way to school in affluent neighborhoods do not stumble over drug paraphernalia. Drive-by shootings do not happen in affluent neighborhoods.

The same is not true of poor neighborhoods, where the drug culture can have devastating effects on parents' attempts to make decent lives for themselves and their children. It is precisely in poor neighborhoods that the restoration of freedom of association and strict property rights offer salvation.

When I mentioned a few chapters back that landlords should discriminate, one issue I had in mind was the drug problem. Landlords, so much maligned, are actually a force for social good because of this one undoubted characteristic: They want responsible tenants who pay their rent on time and don't trash the property. Given their way, they tend to let good tenants be and to evict bad ones, and this is one of the most efficient forms of socialization known to a free society.

The process whereby landlords and tenants find each other is rich in social functions. Entire neighborhoods were once living embodiments of an intricate process whereby norms evolved. Expectations were set up among both landlords and prospective tenants, and money was often a relatively small part of the story. In Harlem in the 1940s the difference between the scruffy, hustling neighborhoods and the exactingly neat and orderly working-class neighborhoods was seldom a great difference in income among the tenants but a difference in norms and values. In the working-class neighborhoods, unless you presented yourself as being a certain kind of person, you weren't going to get in, even if you could pay the rent. In the scruffy neighborhoods you could get in, but landlords charged a premium to compensate for the damage they expected you to cause. Economists have technical descriptions for the equilibria that were reached, but the process was not really so different from the way in which human beings everywhere have historically tended to stratify themselves—not just according to money, but according to tastes and values. In the language I have used throughout the book, they used the process of affiliation.

In the rush to rid society of the socially disapproved reasons for discriminating among rental applicants, starting with race, we threw out as well all the ways in which landlords performed a neighborhood-formation function. It became impossible for a landlord to say with impunity, "I'm not going to rent to you because I don't want you living on my property," which is often what neighborhood-forming decisions have to be based on. Then, to make certain that maintaining cohesive neighborhoods in low-income areas became as difficult as possible, we tore down some of those cohesive neighborhoods in the name of urban renewal, threw up public housing in the middle of other such neighborhoods, and in a variety of ways made it difficult for neighborhoods to define and defend themselves.

In the neighborhoods hardest hit by drugs getting rid of the antidiscrimination laws would make it possible once more for landlords to choose among prospective tenants without having to justify their arbitrariness. If they want to impose a no-drugs rule, they may. If they want to impose a nobody-who-can't-prove-he-has-steady-job rule, they may. If they want to impose a no-welfare-mothers rule, they may. If they don't want to rent to you because they don't like your looks, that's up to them. If a tenant violates the terms of the lease, he may be evicted promptly.

The most effective anti-drugs-in-the-neighborhood policy? Restoration of unrestricted freedom of association and complete deregulation of housing. Give low-income neighborhoods, especially inner-city black neighborhoods, where the drug problem is most concentrated, the freedom to segregate themselves into enclaves, using nonmonetary assets—character and behavior—as the medium of exchange. The solution is not to put all the drug dealers in jail but to enable people to construct neighborhoods which drug dealers will avoid.

7

But what about the full-page, glossy ads for cocaine that we will see in *The New Yorker* if we legalize drugs? Golf tournaments sponsored by marijuana companies? The brightly packaged heroin packets next to the checkout counter at the Seven-Eleven?

The nation has a history in this regard: From the founding through the first decade of the twentieth century, such drugs as cocaine and opium derivatives were legal. These products were openly advertised. But the nation did not have a "drug problem" remotely comparable to today's. Some people misused these drugs and spent much of their time in a stupor (alcohol being the main culprit). But it was not a problem that dragged down civil life in general.

Today the pertinent comparison is probably pornography. Pornography is legal. To my knowledge there is no law preventing porn magazines from taking out full-page color ads in *The New Yorker* or sponsoring golf tournaments. But it doesn't happen. The forces that keep it from happening are the ones that will shape the evolution of drug marketing in an America where drugs are legalized.

I cannot predict in detail how that evolution will take place, but one may be sure of a few things. The crimes that drug users commit will still be crimes. Sitting at home getting high won't be against the law, but robbing someone while you're high will be. Police will be freed to concentrate on catching people who rob people, prosecutors will be freed to concentrate on prosecuting them, and jail cells will be freed to accommodate them. Inner city teenagers will no longer find that the bottom rung of the drug-dealing ladder is more lucrative than the bottom rung of the legitimate job ladder.

Most important, people will begin to deal with drugs as they now deal with alcohol. Alcohol is not a single drug but a variety of products with various uses that are shaped and constrained by a complex matrix of social pressures, conventions, and taboos. Alcohol is a source of pleasure and a source of problems. Its use and misuse go through cycles that have less to do with laws than with cultural shifts. As I write, the use of hard liquor has been steadily declining, moderation is fashionable as well as healthy, and the supports for people who are trying to stop drinking are more widespread and effective than ever before, through associations and mechanisms that are overwhelmingly private. I do not know how long those trends will continue, but when they shift, it will not be for reasons that the government can prevent by force. The best thing that can happen to drug use is that it be brought once again within the social arena where it belongs. Its criminalization has been at least as disastrous for society as a whole as was the criminalization of alcohol in the 1920s.

The generic arguments I have used for the drug case apply as well to prostitution, pornography, and any of the other voluntary, noncoercive human activities that fall under the police label of vice. All of these will be subject to complex social control. Let social control be the mechanism rather than the government's police power.

Protecting the Environment

THE PROPOSAL: *Government sets and enforces minimum standards for air and water quality but does not dictate how those standards are to be met. On other environmental issues all individuals are subject to common law regarding nuisances, and all levels of government are required to observe the Fifth Amendment of the Constitution.*

Environmental issues often conflate private interests and public goods. Some environmental issues involve public goods, classically construed, and warrant a role for government. Other such issues involve a clash of private interests, and are best settled privately.

1

Many environmental complaints are readily resolved in a society that observes property rights and common law. If the factory next door begins emitting noxious fumes onto your property, it has committed a nuisance in common law. You are entitled to relief, enforced by the state. The same holds true for other environmental nuisances. If I build a house on beach property in such a way that it causes the sand dunes on the adjoining property to deteriorate, I can be held liable.

We will worry about more complicated cases in a moment, but it is good to begin by remembering that not everything affects the global ecosystem, or even the ecosystem ten miles down the road. Most disagreements involving the environment are discrete and contained, affecting only a limited sphere in which small numbers of parties are trying to live together harmoniously. All that government needs to do in these cases is to run an efficient civil court, where complaints can be heard promptly and inexpensively.

2

The next, more complicated type of environmental issue affects many property owners—this time the noxious fumes go all over town. To complicate matters, the nuisance is caused jointly by many smokestacks. The transaction costs of solving the problem through common law become so high that the tort solution no longer works. In other words, something valuable (clean air), jointly consumable and not easily segmented, has been degraded. The protection of the clean air has become an authentic public good, and under these circumstances government legitimately acts as a forum for deciding how clean is clean enough and for crafting legislation to produce the desired result.

3

The government's function here is theoretically legitimate. The way in which government has heretofore gone about this function has been ridiculous. Standards for clean air and clean water have been set that exalt purity for purity's sake, independent of real health considerations. Issues of cost have been ignored. National rules have been imposed willy-nilly on local conditions where they don't apply. Emotion has overruled systematic analysis, resulting in measures that have reduced one kind of pollution at the cost of producing more and worse kinds of collateral pollution.

What are the principles for environmental regulation that will protect people from real environmental harms while restraining the government from intruding where it has no business? Here are five that will make a good start:

BASE ENVIRONMENTAL STANDARDS ON OUTCOMES, NOT ACTIVITIES. Environmental legislation often tries to prescribe not only the level of emissions to be permitted but also the technology that industries must employ to reach that level. This asks bureaucracies to do what they are worst at—be innovative. Private industry has powerful incentives to meet environmental standards with as little disruption to its activities and costs as possible; it will therefore energetically search out new technologies, new manufacturing setups, innovations of all kinds. Government's job is to do a hard-headed assessment of the science of the situation and to decide, through an open and deliberative process, what level of emissions or contaminants is acceptable. Then get out of the way.

CREATE TRADEABLE POLLUTION RIGHTS UNDER A CAP. The cost of reducing pollution by a given amount can vary drastically from industry to industry, process to process, and company to company. Suppose it is going to cost a company A $20 million to reduce its sulfur dioxide emission levels by one unit, but it will cost a company *B* only $1 million dollars to do the same thing. Let company *A* pay company *B* to reduce its sulfur dioxide so that the net amount of sulfur dioxide produced by two firms remains under a cap that the government has set. To date such trading has been permitted in a few cases under formidable restrictions. Open up the process, get rid of the restrictions, and let the market work.

APPLY THE PRINCIPLE OF SUBSIDIARITY. A smokestack in a town in North Dakota, where it is the only smokestack within a hundred miles, need not be subject to the same regulation as a smokestack in Pittsburgh, where it is one of dozens within a few square miles. Let cities deal with city-wide problems and states deal with state-wide problems. For the federal government to get involved, it is not enough to prove that molecules of Pennsylvania air drift across the border into Maryland; an authentic public good has to be at stake, based on evidence, in a case that cannot be resolved by the parties involved.

The reason for applying the principle of subsidiarity is partly to preserve freedom. Some environmental issues require a loss of individual freedom in the service of a public good, but such losses should be taken seriously and minimized. The principle of subsidiarity serves that end. But it also serves the interests of justice and equity. Millions of people have chosen to live in places that have warm weather and pretty scenery but where it is exceedingly expensive to maintain a livable environment. The Los Angeles area in particular, with 6 percent of the nation's population trying to live in an arid bowl, poses horrendous environmental problems. If people want to live in Los Angeles, that's their business. The rest of the nation should not have to live by the rules that Los Angeles needs nor subsidize the costs that are properly borne by the people who enjoy the benefits of living in Los Angeles. A fair environmental policy must make sure that Peter is not permitted to get clean air by forcing Paul to pay for it.

GET THE COSTS RIGHT, AND MAKE THE COSTS VISIBLE. If you ask people whether they want five particles or one particle of a contaminant per thousand units of water, people will vote for one. If you tell people that they have a choice of paying a water rate of $1 or $5 per thousand units of water, they will vote for $1. Government must tell the citizenry and their elected representatives how those two choices interact—what they're buying with the extra $4; what it will cost to eliminate the extra four particles. Then make people pay accordingly, in the form of taxes, rather than hiding the cost in unfunded mandates.

DEPOLITICIZE THE SCIENCE. The environmental movement is dominated by people who tend to be hostile to free markets, technology, and economic growth. The result has been a great deal of bad science and spurious interpretations of good science. If we really wanted to reduce the injuries, deaths, and pollution required to produce electricity, for example, the science of the matter is clear: We would shift to nuclear power forthwith. If the test of a recycling program is whether it reduces waste and saves energy, the science is again clear: Most recycling programs flunk. But the science in these cases works against the environmental movement's ethos, and it is ignored.

I know of no libertarian measures for depoliticizing science. In the long run truth wins in science, and presumably that will happen sooner or later with regard to the environment. The process will be hurried along by putting the costs of environmental fixes up front. Environmental measures based on bad data would get a much more searching examination if the costs to the taxpayer were openly stated and directly charged.

4

Once we move beyond clean air and water into issues involving the wilderness, endangered species, and wetlands, we have to stop and recognize the dirty little secret of American environmentalism: Much of it represents the aesthetics and ethics of a particular segment of American society—a segment that also happens to be extremely powerful. Many environmental measures represent class interests in disguise and involve no public goods worthy of the name.

It is difficult even to discuss this issue, because adamancy about the environment has become so great. *Of course* wilderness areas must be preserved and endangered species protected at whatever cost; *of course* recyclable goods must be recycled at whatever inconvenience—these are seen not as idiosyncratic agendas, but as revealed truth. I do not use the phrase *revealed truth* carelessly. Among America's secular elites the politics of environmentalism resemble religious evangelism.

A thought experiment will illustrate what I mean by class interests. Imagine a Congress of the United States that is composed entirely of blue-collar workers and farmers. I stipulate that they are just as intelligent and devoted to the public good as the Members of Congress they replace. But most of these new Members have spent their adult lives as construction workers, factory workers, truck drivers, and electricians. They identify with blue-collar neighborhoods, blue-collar incomes, and blue-collar recreations. The rest of this Congress are farmers who know the environment not as an abstraction or an ideal but as a day-to-day reality of their working lives. Let us imagine this new Congress as it turns to the latest proposals for environmental law.

Protect endangered species? A Congress of blue-collar workers and farmers is unlikely to hold up a dam to save the snail darter or throw several hundred loggers out of work to protect the spotted owl. Such a Congress is unlikely to pass a law that lets the government prevent a farmer from farming his land because a patch of Cuyamaca meadow-foam grows on it.

Let a developer build a new shopping center on wetlands? An upper-middle-class Congress tends to see a new shopping center as urban sprawl. A blue-collar Congress is more likely to see it as a convenient place for people to shop. And if the shopping center is to be built on land with a high water table—now officially labeled *wetlands*—a blue-collar Congress will ask more critically than will an upper-middle-class Congress, "What's the real harm of filling in fifty acres of soggy ground?"

Protect wilderness areas? Environmentalists work diligently to close off large sections of the national parks to anyone except backpackers. But it also happens that the people who backpack are disproportionately people who have money, time, and flexibility about when they take vacations and what they do with the kids. The people who are hurt by closing off much of the national parks tend to be working-class people who do not have much money or free time, are required to take their vacations in the first two weeks in August, and have three kids in the camper. A blue-collar Congress is going to be a lot less sympathetic than an upper-middle-class Congress to the Secretary of the Interior when he tries to explain the new restrictions.

Who is right? The Congress we have now or the Congress of blue-collar workers and farmers? Neither. Many of the currently fashionable environmental positions are arbitrary, and the different rules set by a Congress of blue-collar workers and farmers would be equally arbitrary. Enforcing them would be equally a matter of people's gaining control of the police power to get what they want at the expense of others.

5

The first part of a general solution for environmental issues involving aesthetics and ethics is to apply the nuisance rule of common law. If no nuisance is inflicted on me, what you do with your property is none of my business. That I do not approve of your taste does not give me the right to enlist the police on my side.

This rule will leave some issues hotly contested. If I live in a small town where someone wants to open a strip mine, perhaps I will be eager for the mine because I want to apply for a job, or perhaps I will oppose the mine because it will ruin the view from my home. The nuisance question will have to be fought out, and people who are damaged by the strip mine will have to be compensated. But as matters stand, we live in a nation where people who will never get within hundreds of miles of the strip mine have the right to make the decision for the people involved. Leaving the decision in the hands of those who stand to gain and lose most directly will resolve the vast majority of cases equitably.

6

The second part of the solution to issues of competing aesthetics and ethics is to enforce the clause in the Fifth Amendment of the Constitution that states, "nor shall private property be taken for public use, without just compensation." Take and pay.

As a practical matter many disputes over aesthetics and ethics are going to fall into a gray area where a public good might be discerned that justifies government action. Is preserving an endangered species a public good? As a libertarian I am willing to say unequivocally that preserving Cuyamaca meadow-foam does not qualify. But preserving the bald eagle from extinction? A lower-case libertarian like me has to hedge on that one, and when measures are passed to insure that a habitat for the bald eagle is preserved, I will not march on Washington in opposition. But if saving bald eagles is a public good, it has to be paid for by everyone, not just by people who happen to own land where bald eagles nest. If preserving beach dunes is a public good, everyone has to chip in to buy them or to compensate their owners for being denied permission to use their property as they wish.

In this arena case law has become a travesty as courts have found elaborate excuses to deny that a taking has occurred. I propose a simple construction of the Fifth Amendment. The baseline assumption is that people may do whatever they wish with their own property, subject to conventional tort law. Any additional governmental restrictions on the use of privately owned property in the name of a public good constitutes a taking and must be compensated.

7

In recent years the environment has almost escaped the reach of rational discourse. Hardly any other issue is as fraught with fears that apocalypse is upon us unless the government steps in.

The facts about protection of the environment are so far at odds with the conventional wisdom that it is hard to know where to begin. This book is not the proper place to argue out these complicated empirical controversies. Some sources listed in the bibliographic essay provide a good start. I will assert—and I invite you to explore the assertion for yourself—that government has not been the great protector of wilderness and wildlife that the environmental orthodoxy portrays it to be. Private landowners have not been the great despoilers that the environmental orthodoxy portrays them to be.

More broadly: Strict property rights, *extended* rather than limited, offer our best hope for protecting the environment. Stewardship is one of the things that private property owners do best.

Removing Government from Civil Life

THE PROPOSAL: *Eliminate all governmental social-service programs and all income transfers in cash or kind.*

Poverty has been the natural human state throughout history. It remains so for most of the world's population today. Over the course of the twentieth century a few industrialized nations have arrived at a destination unique in human history: They have enough national wealth to grant everyone the means to live a decent material existence.

This developing capability has been one of freedom's great enemies. The goal of an end to poverty is so noble that governments have successfully used the end to justify the means. The means have been high taxation of the productive members of society and arrays of bureaucracies that increasingly regulate the lives of us all.

1

The first step for libertarians is to acknowledge, freely and without reservation, the nobility of the goal. It is distressing when want exists amid plenty, and humans have a moral obligation to do what they can. Or as one wise man put it, "He is certainly not a good citizen who does not wish to promote, by every means in his power, the welfare of the whole society of his fellow citizens." That is Adam Smith talking, the apostle of laissez-faire. This injunction applies not merely to poverty but to all the human predicaments that arise from the randomness of life and lead us to say, "There but for the grace of God go I." To some extent life is indeed a lottery, just as the social democrats insist.

That chance plays a large role in life is not news, but it needs to be emphasized because the political debate has tended to push libertarians into unnecessarily extreme positions. The idea that we are our brothers' keepers has been used so flabbily, for so many destructive schemes, that one has a strong impulse to say, "The hell I am." But the Bible cannot be held responsible for its misuse by twentieth-century politicians, and the whining of some social democrats that no one is responsible for his fate should not provoke libertarians into saying that anyone can stand on his own two feet if he has a little gumption. We all need a little help from our friends, and some of us need a great deal. What becomes of those who are helpless, or luckless, or perhaps simply feckless, must deeply concern any human being worthy of the name. So say all of the world's great religious traditions. So say the great thinkers in the classical liberal tradition. So say most of their followers, including me.

Should government be the instrument for discharging this obligation?

2

You know all the reasons for answering yes. They have been the received wisdom since the New Deal. Only the government can make certain that everyone is helped. The job is too big and too important to be left to the whims of individuals. Charity is degrading. The poor and needy should have help as a matter of social justice. Wealth must be fairly distributed.

In contrast, I will state briefly what I and many other libertarians believe:

The phenomenal growth in national wealth during this century should have left the United States with only a tiny proportion of the population in poverty. As of the 1990s America should be a place in which virtually everyone has enough income to provide for bad times, old age, and medical care; a place where virtually everyone takes for granted that he must support the children he brings into the world; a place where virtually everyone grows up expecting that his first duty in life is to be self-supporting and where he is equipped with the social and job skills to do so.

As of the 1990s America should be a place in which the small remainder of the population—whether these people be helpless, luckless, or feckless—have ample sources of support from a wealthy nation that retains the tradition of private generosity and helping associations that has been its hallmark from the beginning.

America is not that place. The entry of government into social insurance and then into a broader range of social interventions has caused incalculable human suffering. It has not produced a society in which fewer people are dependent than would otherwise have been the case. The welfare state has artificially, needlessly created a large dependent class. At the bottom is the underclass, stripped of dignity and autonomy, producing new generations socialized to their parents' behavior.

There is no excuse for what has happened except the excuse of good intentions, and even that is a lame one. To justify the creation of the welfare state, politicians and intellectuals had to ignore commentaries on human nature from modern psychology back to the ancients. They had to ignore the results of earlier attempts that plainly foreshadowed what would happen if such systems were tried again on a larger scale. They had to ignore early indications after the first welfare legislation passed that their good intentions would backfire.

That America is not the land of universal plenty it should have become is for many libertarians, including me, the source of our deepest anger about what big government has done to this country.

3

But what should have been and could have been did not materialize. Given the reality facing us today, what is to be done?

The answer depends on what we want to accomplish. Like most libertarians I do not consider reducing poverty the top priority of a civilized society. Protecting human freedom is. But many social-welfare policies leave an acceptable, if not perfect, level of human freedom. In choosing among the tolerable alternatives, the criterion of success is that human needs—unmet material needs as well as unmet needs of the spirit—fall to as low a level as possible.

That last phrase, "as low a level as possible," is the stinger. There can be no such thing as a society free of human suffering. No matter what social and economic system is put in place, some proportion of children will be neglected, some adults will be desperately lonely, some people will suffer terrible accidents and diseases that leave them incapacitated, and some people will live in squalor.

In responding to this reality, the first requirement is to recognize that it is indeed a reality. Much of our debate about social policy ignores it. A libertarian solution cannot fairly be criticized for acknowledging openly that some level of human suffering will remain. Suffering will remain in all systems. The only difference is in the comparative amounts of the different kinds.

The second requirement is to understand that different kinds of human suffering cannot be put into neat boxes that permit us to deal with one problem without affecting another. The ways in which people acquire satisfactions in life, or fail to acquire them, is intimately bound up in the way that they provide for their material well-being.

Then all of us, libertarian or social democrat, conservative or liberal, have a common test to put to our prescriptions for dealing with social problems: *Am I convinced that if my plan is adopted, the net effect will be less suffering and human need than would exist under any alternative I can think of?*

4

Even for libertarians, governmental social insurance can be an option. Two of the greatest classical liberals of the twentieth century, Friedrich Hayek and Milton Friedman, accept the idea that some limited form of government social insurance is appropriate. Most current libertarian discussions of the issue involve proposals to improve the current system without eradicating it altogether—privatizing Social Security, devolving welfare programs to the states, establishing medical savings accounts to replace Medicare, and the like.

I have been drawn to Milton Friedman's argument for a negative income tax (NIT) that entirely replaces the existing system of income transfers and social services. The quid pro quo would be that the government withdraw altogether from every other form of interference in the organization of social life. Under such a plan the Department of Health and Human Services would become a check-writing office, and the social service agencies, bureaus, and offices scattered throughout government would close down. For five years I have had in my desk drawer a finished manuscript explaining the reasons for concluding that such a system is affordable and would have more good effects than bad. A version of it survived to a late draft of this book.

The main attraction of a generous NIT is that it could resolve an impasse. As matters stand, every element of limited government now faces a blanket objection: But what about poor people? An NIT could take poverty off the table by giving every adult an income above the poverty line. Doing so is probably the single most important step in getting the nation to think seriously about restoring limited government. The left has always claimed it wanted to end material poverty. A generous NIT would do that. Is the left willing to give up the apparatus of the welfare state in return?

But the NIT fails the ultimate question: Am I convinced that if my plan is adopted, the net effect will be less suffering and human need than would exist under any alternative I can think of? I cannot think of a better politically realistic alternative than the NIT. But I can think of one that would produce less net human suffering.

5

End governmental transfer payments, in cash, kind, or services. Do not substitute less coercive government programs for the ones we have now. Do not try to make the best of a bad situation. Dismantle every vestige of the state social-insurance and welfare apparatus and constitutionally forbid its reappearance. I include in this statement every middle-class entitlement, agricultural subsidy, and corporate subsidy along with programs for the poor.

I ask you to think about this future not because I think it will come about in my lifetime but because I think this is the way in which high-technology, advanced societies will eventually find that they work best for the happiness of all the people.

6

You may imagine whatever transitional mechanism you wish—a ten-year warning period, continuation of benefits for people already on the welfare system without allowing new entrants, a one-time option to stay in the Social Security system (and keep paying FICA taxes) and to stay in Medicare (and keep paying FICAMED). My interest focuses on what happens afterward.

One reflexive answer is that, afterward, the social order collapses. The babies of the poor languish. Poor people, lacking places to live, huddle in cardboard boxes beneath overpasses. The rich install ever more sophisticated security systems around their estates. But of course that is not a prediction about what happens after we get rid of the social insurance system. *That is what's happening now.* It was not always true in America that the children of the poor were neglected, that those without homes lived in boxes, and that the rich needed elaborate security systems. It need not be true in the future.

7

Earlier in the book I mentioned the intimate relationship between freedom and responsibility in producing human satisfactions and enjoyments. Here, we revisit that theme from another perspective.

Social policy seeks certain results: People who are not poor. Children who are loved and nurtured. Access to health care. Low crime. High employment. At a more ambitious level, social policy seeks to promote a society characterized by compassion, generosity, and tolerance. Under the surface all of these outcomes are produced by two elemental particles—freedom and responsibility—combined into different molecules.

Responsibility—knowing that our actions have consequences for our lives and the lives of our loved ones— carries the primary load. It is the prospect of consequences that shapes the lessons our parents teach us as toddlers. It is the prospect of consequences that underwrites the authority of moral precepts. It is the refusal to accept the link between our behavior and consequences that accounts for many of the mistakes that, in the long term, can ruin a life.

Freedom's role as an elemental particle is to expand the voluntary and cooperative options for dealing with consequences. As an example take provision for old age. Every human culture devises ways for dealing with old age. In primitive cultures dealing with old age can mean putting the aged out in the snow. In traditional peasant cultures it can mean cultural norms that demand a filial loyalty so overriding as to stifle human initiative and creativity. In a free society people have many ways of dealing with old age. They tend to take one from each column: save for the future, find a spouse who will be a helpmeet, affiliate with others in one's craft or profession who provide mutual help, be a part of a community that takes care of its own. Freedom opens up these multiple strategies. It also creates a cultural climate that rejects fatalism and embraces the idea that people can arrange for their own care. In the earlier discussion of the pursuit of happiness, I wrote that to take personal responsibility infuses freedom with life. Here, I am arguing that freedom makes it much easier for people to make good on their personal responsibilities.

Freedom and responsibility form different combinations in different parts of life, producing results as apparently unlike as helium and lead. Here are some of them, when government no longer interferes:

8

Knowing that they must be responsible for their own futures, people take a hard look at their retirement situations. Savings rates skyrocket. With high savings rates go economic advantages that make the entire national economy sounder, wealthier, more competitive.

Just about everyone who has a job *can* save. FICA and FICAMED, taxes that begin at the bottom of the wage ladder, disappear. The maximum income tax rate falls to single digits. The $1 trillion a year no longer spent on the programs I want to eliminate is not thrown into the ocean; it remains in the pockets of the people who earned it, to be spent, invested in productive enterprises, and contributed to the welfare of their fellow citizens as they see fit.

Knowing that they must be responsible for their own futures, people do something so human that it is a cliché: They make a virtue of necessity. Social signals and social rewards are transformed. The simple act of taking care of yourself and your family once again becomes a credential that cuts across economic and ethnic divisions and takes on a value that transcends economics. To be a young man and out of the labor force is once again to be a bum. The poor are once again divided into the deserving and the undeserving, based on whether people are suffering from misfortunes beyond their control or have brought their troubles on themselves. It turns out that this system gives ordinary people, otherwise undistinguished, an avenue for gaining the respect of those around them. You do not have to be rich to have dignity, to elicit from other people a recognition that you are a solid citizen, a substantial person, regardless of your income. All you have to do is pull your own weight, or even make a good-faith effort.

Knowing that they must be responsible for their own futures, people think about marriage differently. Marriage becomes less about living with an attractive companion until you get bored and more about securing the social and economic foundations of the rest of one's life. Your partner's qualities can make the difference between security and comfort or a precarious subsistence, between a fulfilling place in the community and a barren one. The penalties of a bad marital choice and the rewards of a good one both multiply. A woman who, apart from everything else, has to worry about being left holding the baby looks at men accordingly. She raises the value she attaches to such qualities as integrity, fidelity, industriousness, and the skills to make a living. Men, as they always have, try to acquire whatever qualities will make them attractive to women.

Knowing that they must be responsible for their own futures, far fewer women allow themselves to have a baby without a husband. The penalties for doing so become huge, immediate, and so pressing that they cannot be ignored. The crushing financial burden of a baby is the most tangible penalty, but there are social ones as well. The stigma against single motherhood quickly makes a comeback: Until the government began masking the social costs created by large numbers of fatherless children, civilized communities everywhere stigmatized illegitimacy. The revived stigma also means that a single mother has drastically devalued her stock in the marriage market at a time when the marriage market has become more important. For it works both ways: The honest and hardworking men who have become more desirable as husbands are looking for wives, and such men tend to want women who are honorable, faithful, and responsible. This kind of appraisal works against the woman who has had a baby without the means to care for it.

Knowing that they must be responsible for their own futures, people once again see their families as units that offer protections against the vicissitudes of life. But for a family to function in that way, children must grow up accepting their obligations toward their parents and siblings. They must grow up expecting to work and knowing how to work. These realities affect the way parents raise their children, generally leading them to elevate the importance of inculcating virtue. Childhood and adolescence are treated as preparation for a life filled with responsibility. This way of raising children has important practical benefits for the parents. It also has a side effect: It produces children who grow up healthier, wiser, and happier than their counterparts who grew up in the welfare state.

9

This account is not pulled from thin air. It describes the prevailing norms of personal and family behavior that existed in an America without a government safety net. This is the way it was—not for every single person in the country, but as the overwhelmingly dominant ethic.

What kind of a culture does this ethic produce? Not a Puritan one—Puritan cultures are filled with responsibility but not with freedom. The history of the United States from the Revolution through the 1920s records that America under limited government had no shortage of hellraising and good times, quirky individualism and bohemian enclaves. America had a vital culture that was rich in literature, art, philosophy, and music—richer and more vital, one might argue, than American culture today. In ridding ourselves of the welfare state, I am thinking first about the building blocks of a free society, confident that its rewards will be not only a society that is prosperous and virtuous, but one that is exciting and fun as well.

10

America under a restored limited government will also be a society with far greater texture, far less anomie and alienation than now. If you want to end the atomization of modern life, get government out of it. The only way people can afford to be atomized is if the government subsidizes it.

This, too, is more than wishful thinking. It is confirmed by everything we know about our history. Americans are a people who relish association—clubs, fraternal organizations, associations for the preservation of everything from wildlife to battlefields, associations for assistance to everyone from widows and orphans to teamsters and the Sons of Italy. Alexis de Tocqueville was among the first to marvel at the American genius for voluntary associations, but he was not the last.

I am not talking about such quasi-governmental bureaucracies as the United Way and the Red Cross but about the associations that are hardly visible to official Washington though they form an important part of daily life elsewhere in America. The Rotarians, Kiwanians, Ruritanians. The Elk, Moose, Oddfellows. Little League. Junior League. Boy Scouts and Girl Scouts. The PTA. The tens of thousands of committees in churches and synagogues. The roster of American voluntary associations that still survive would take a much longer book than this merely to list.

Coupled with this political heritage is an American tradition of generosity. From the time of the first settlements Americans made provision for the poor and their children. The small-town tradition of helping carried over to large cities. Even in the early nineteenth century, philanthropic societies for the assistance of the poor were already at work in New York, Boston, and the other major American cities. By the end of the nineteenth century America's philanthropic system showed us a glimpse of how vital and effective private philanthropy could be today. American charity for the poor did not consist of a few Lady Bountifuls with food baskets but formed an extensive and sophisticated system of private charities, friendly societies, private insurance, and mutual-aid associations that did an extraordinary job, *given the level of national wealth at that time,* of dealing with the problems of poverty and economic security. Yes, there was terrible poverty in the great cities in the nineteenth century. But there was terrible poverty everywhere. The norm in the countryside was poverty as well. In Europe rural poverty was even more grinding than it was in the cities. That's why immigrants flocked to America. The story of American slums of the nineteenth century is not that they existed but how they transformed themselves into thriving communities.

11

The obstacle to getting rid of government transfers is not a reasoned analysis of the outcomes but psychological self-protection. The reality is that right now millions of Americans are experiencing precisely the kinds of suffering that people predict will happen if we get rid of the welfare state. Millions of adults and children alike suffer from neglect, abuse, and stunted cognitive and emotional development—phenomena that were not inevitable but were subsidized and fostered by the welfare state. But because we are spending so much government money to solve these problems, however ineffectually and counterproductively, we can comfort ourselves that "At least we're trying." Libertarians just want to give up, it is said.

No. Libertarians want a society in which people find dignity and a role in life by supporting themselves. Libertarians want a society in which far greater proportions of children than now come into the world with two responsible, committed parents who will give them a decent chance at life. Libertarians want a society in which, when parents fail, there are strong social institutions surrounding the child—not bureaucracies but extended family, neighbors, church, local philanthropies—people who know the child and can help more effectively than any government program can. Libertarians want actual suffering to decrease, in contrast to grand government plans that are supposed to reduce suffering but produce more.

The genius of free human beings is that, given responsibility, they join together to take care of each other—to be their brothers' keepers when their brother needs help. The triumph of an earlier America was that it had set all the right trends in motion, at a time when the world was first coming out of millennia of poverty into an era of plenty. The tragedy of contemporary America is that it abandoned that course. Libertarians want to return to it.

Loose Ends

IN THIS DISCUSSION of a workable libertarian state I have not tried to deal with every issue but have focused on the ones that seem to me to pose the toughest problems. The approaches I would advocate for issues such as foreign policy, monetary policy, immigration, tax policy, and criminal justice bear a strong family resemblance to the approaches in the discussions you have just read.

For all libertarian solutions, this tension persists: Limited government could work if it were enacted. But it will not be enacted at one time, and partial solutions are often worse than the status quo. We saw what happened when some restrictions on the savings and loan industry were lifted but the government kept its insurance guarantees in place, inviting insurance and loan executives to take wild risks. Legalizing drugs while keeping the welfare state in place would be similarly ill-advised. There is nothing magic about "less government" unless people understand why less government works. I propose a First Law of Libertarian Reform that reads: *Every increase in freedom of action must be matched with a corresponding increase in responsibility for consequences.*

Politicians are among the least likely people to understand that law. Fortunately, most advocates of limited government understand it as an integral part of their philosophy, and they have developed proposals for incremental reforms that observe it. The discussion in the previous

chapters often passed over the options for incremental reform in favor of the complete solution. That doesn't mean
that incremental reforms can't be steps in the right direction. The problem is to find voting majorities that will
support them—the issue to which I now turn.

IS IT POSSIBLE?

*In which are considered
the circumstances under which limited
government might be restored.*

Gloom and Hope

A LEGITIMATE QUESTION: Why bother laying out the parameters of a limited government that is so politically unrealistic?

Strict constitutional limits on the government's power? The United States electorate wouldn't approve even the Bill of Rights if it were put up for a vote. Polls have asked.

Get rid of Social Security and Medicare? The electorate is terrified by the prospect of reductions in the *rate of growth* of Social Security and Medicare.

End regulation of products and services? An iron triangle of politicians, big business, and consumer groups have achieved a modus vivendi that serves each of their interests.

Restore freedom of association? Not a single major figure in public life supports unrestricted freedom of association.

Limited government in twenty-first-century America? Surely nothing resembling the state I outlined has any chance of being enacted.

LOOKING AT WHERE WE ARE, pessimism is realistic. Looking at where we are going, a libertarian has real reason to hope. Tectonic shifts in the American polity are underway. Where they will take us and how fast is obscure. But the potential for change is enormous.

Government As "Them"

THE PROPOSITION: *When American government is no longer "us" but "them," large changes become possible.*

When Lyndon Johnson took office, about 75 percent of Americans said that they trusted the federal government. Now about 75 percent respond to the same polling question by saying that they do not trust the federal government. Every other survey of public attitudes toward government shows the same kind of alienation. Only an insignificant fraction of these responses comes from extremists with their militias and conspiracy theories. Overwhelmingly they are the responses of ordinary, thoughtful people who no longer see government as an ally.

The conventional academic wisdom is that this alienation is temporary, part of a cyclical phenomenon. Historians point out that the United States has always swung from involvement in public affairs to disengagement, from liberalism to conservatism, then back again, in cycles that last decades. The nation is in a conservative phase now; it will move back to a liberal phase.

I propose another explanation: The reason so many Americans have become alienated from government since the poll of 1964 is that government really has become more incompetent and really has become alienated from the public it is supposed to serve. Political cycles and political fashion have nothing to do with it. American government isn't what it used to be.

1

For 150 years American government limited itself to a few things that everyone agreed government ought to do, and government did them pretty well. The Post Office delivered the mail. The Army won its wars. Police caught criminals. Judges put them in jail. Fire departments put out fires.

Since 1933, and accelerating after 1964, three things changed this state of affairs. The government began trying to do many more things. Government began to do almost everything less well. Private alternatives sprang up. The three events are not unrelated.

THE GOVERNMENT BEGAN TRYING TO DO MANY MORE THINGS and quickly ran out of things that it knows how to do. The old functions of government were straightforward. Some of them were not easy tasks, but they were *known* tasks, with by-the-book techniques that worked. A bureaucracy could do them. In contrast, healing an abused child is not a known task. Instilling racial understanding is not a known task. Teaching self-restraint to teenagers is not a known task. Good people try to achieve such goals in the course of their lives, sometimes succeeding, sometimes failing. But the tasks have no by-the-book procedures. Bureaucracies make a mess of them.

THE GOVERNMENT BEGAN DOING ITS OLD JOBS LESS WELL. Old roles were burdened with new tasks. The cop was supposed to be a social worker now as well as someone who catches criminals. The teacher was supposed to be a social worker as well as an educator of students. The new tasks competed with the core functions. Less time, less intensity, less motivation were devoted to the core functions.

The new tasks took moral priority. If the government is

trying to do fifty things of high social purpose, keeping the streets clean has a low priority. Can a mayor cut the budget for the drug rehabilitation program to buy ten more street cleaning vehicles? It's tough, because rescuing human beings is more important in the cosmic scheme of things than is cleaning streets. Never mind if the government doesn't actually succeed in rescuing the human beings, and never mind if the streets are dirty. It's the thought that counts. Once government began to see its role as doing good, the sense of what government does well got lost, overwhelmed by the sense of what government ought to *try* to do.

PRIVATE ALTERNATIVES SPRANG UP. As the government tried to do more and did it worse, the private sector built parallel systems doing the same thing that the government does. Faxes, e-mail, and the overnight mail services increasingly let us bypass the Post Office. Private security forces, electronic security systems, and gated communities let us isolate ourselves from the breakdown of law in the streets. Corporations sidestep an increasingly Dickensian court system by arranging to arbitrate disagreements through private judges. Families choose private schools instead of public ones.

2

As government does more things worse and as private alternatives expand, comparisons between the public and private sectors become increasingly embarrassing to the government. In one part of our lives—the part run by private enterprises—we have become accustomed to a level of responsiveness and service that is often astonishing. We can order just about any product from our home, expect it to show up on our doorstep the next day, and take it for granted that if we don't like it we can return it, no questions asked. We go to shopping centers that are a combination of Taj Mahal and amusement park and that are cleaner, safer, and more pleasant than the public streets. We listen to dire warnings about the power of multinational corporations on C-SPAN, but our interaction with these entities really consists of their politely begging us to buy their cars and televisions and computers, which are offered with more functions, higher quality, and more competitive prices than ever before.

In another part of our lives, the part run by government, we have to fill out our tax returns, renew our driver's license, try to get a pothole fixed, try to correct an overcharge in the water bill, try to get an answer to a question about the zoning laws, or apply for a permit. Something that in the private sector can be done in minutes over the phone, 24 hours a day, can be done by the government only from ten until three, Mondays through Fridays, in person, and it takes three visits to get it right. That overcharge in the water bill? You end up paying it, because if you persist, a confused water department will probably turn off your water for nonpayment.

Americans aren't imagining these differences between the private world and the public world. They look around and ask themselves what works and what doesn't. What is beautiful and what is ugly. Who is courteous and who is rude. Where it is tidy and where it is not. The reality of daily life is that, by and large, the things the government does tend to be ugly, rude, slovenly—and not to work. Things that private organizations do tend to be attractive, courteous, tidy—and to work. That is the way America really is.

3

The growing incompetence of government is not subject to cycles. The public sector will not get better at performing its new tasks, no matter how energetically people try to reinvent government. There are certain things that government is inherently unfitted to do. Nor will the government get better at doing the things it *is* fitted to do unless it divests itself of everything else. The only way that government is going to get better at cleaning streets is if keeping the streets clean is once again one of its few jobs, and one that it takes seriously.

The Demand to Be Left Alone

THE PROPOSITION: *As Americans begin to identify areas of life in which they are willing to give up government benefits in return for being left alone, large changes become possible.*

For years the conventional wisdom has been: "Americans say they want smaller government except when it comes to their own benefits." It may have been true once. It is getting less true every day. The quid pro quo that government wants in return for its favors has grown too large. For an increasing number of Americans the government is more than a nuisance. It keeps them from living the life they correctly feel they have earned the right to live. Politically, most of them probably still identify themselves as moderate Democrats and Republicans. Few have read Hayek or Friedman or Smith. But their lived experience leads them to ask, often with rising passion: Why can't the government just leave me alone?

1

People who run small businesses increasingly want to be left alone. I alluded to their situation in the thought experiment about getting rid of regulation. It is time to elaborate.

The government can demand conformity to exquisitely detailed regulations about the physical arrangement of a business's space, the facilities it includes, the conduct of its work. Government may regulate how much that business charges and the terms under which it bills. Government gets involved in whom a business may hire, how much it pays, and the benefits it provides. The government may make it next to impossible to fire someone without risking a lawsuit. Government may summarily order a business to take actions costing tens of thousands of dollars—millions, in the case of a large business. Government monitors all these demands with a mass of paperwork and an army of enforcers who can disrupt a business with arbitrary decisions. On top of all that are heavy taxes.

What the government does to the people with small businesses is not merely a matter of income. To open one's own business is the archetypal American way of getting ahead and making freedom and independence real. People who run small businesses, or would like to do so, have been impeded not just in making a living but in trying to make a life for themselves. Often the cost is greater than "impeding." Government regulation has prevented many from starting businesses and forced many others to fail.

There are about twenty million corporations, partnerships, and proprietorships with receipts under $1 million, and another million farm owners. This amounts to some forty-plus million people who are directly involved in these enterprises as owners, partners, or spouses. It seems likely that some large proportion of this population would be prepared to give up every government "benefit" in return for being left alone to run their business as they see fit.

2

The parents of elementary- and secondary-school children increasingly want to be left alone. For many the decision has already been made. About five million American children attend private elementary and secondary schools. Another million are being home schooled. Of the forty-four million children enrolled in public schools, polling data indicate that about two-thirds of their parents give American public schools a grade of *C* or worse. More tellingly, about a third of them give a *C* or worse to the school their own child attends.

Most of these dissatisfied parents feel powerless. Until the mid 1960s education was a wholly local function. Whatever parents didn't like about their school they took up with the PTA and the principal, who often had broad discretionary power. If that didn't work, there was the local school board. The closeness of the bond between the parents and schools was not only procedural. The parents were too close, too involved, too vocal for a local school to diverge very far from the parents' ideas about what to teach, how to teach it, and how to deal with disruptive students. Schools reflected the local cultural norms.

Then the Johnson administration began offering money to local public schools. School boards enthusiastically accepted it. But the money had strings—a few at first, then more. The schools soon became dependent on the money and found themselves forced to accept a wide range of restrictions and mandates if the money pipeline was to stay open. These strings reflected the values of the elite culture that created them, and they were often at odds with parents' educational priorities.

At about the same time the federal courts became involved in schooling with a series of sweeping decisions about everything from forced busing on behalf of racial integration to due process for fractious students. Occasionally, as in Boston or Kansas City, the courts seized administrative control over entire school systems. Teachers' unions grew in size and power, and so did the stranglehold they established over work rules and pedagogy in their contracts with school boards. The parents were entirely left out of these changes.

Few of today's dissatisfied parents think they can fix their school's problems. The wealthiest, the most determined, and the most alienated have already said, in effect, "I'll keep on paying for a public-school system and a private one besides, in return for the chance to be left alone." Millions of other dissatisfied parents are looking for ways to increase their control over their children's education, prepared to forego federal assistance if that is the price they must pay.

3

People who are still in the middle of their working lives and thinking about their retirement increasingly want to be left alone to arrange for their own retirement.

Social Security is a Ponzi scheme. People who have been paying into Social Security do not have accounts that the US government holds for them. Their money goes directly to the people already in the system. When there is something left over (as during the 1980s and 1990s, with the baby boomers in their peak earning years), it supposedly goes into a trust fund. But the Social Security trust fund is used to help finance the budget deficit. It consists of

IOUs from the Federal Treasury that will have to be redeemed when they come due.

It won't work. There are too many baby boomers and not enough people in the subsequent generation. Social Security as we know it cannot survive the demographics of the next half-century without tax rates that reach Scandinavian levels.

The coming bankruptcy of the Social Security system is a story that is finally beginning to get the attention it deserves, and the nation is within a few years of a profound political shift. Until now Social Security and Medicare have been the third rail of American politics: Touch it and die. The elderly have been one of America's best-organized political pressure groups and have effectively shut off any serious restraint on their entitlements. The baby boomers, moving into their fifties, will want to protect the system if they can. But voters in their twenties, thirties, and forties already openly doubt that they will ever get their money back when they retire, and they are on the verge of voting their anger.

How many people are upset? As of 1992, 47 million people were in the 18–44 age group and were either householder or spouse in a household making more than $30,000—which means that their household was paying somewhere between $1,800 and $7,600 into FICA every year. All who think that Social Security will go bankrupt will prefer to opt out of the current system. But even if the promised benefits were to be paid, many millions in this group correctly calculate that they would be better off using their FICA taxes to fund their own retirement annuities. If they are left alone, they can experience a comfortable old age. If the government keeps trying to do it for them, they will be worse off. A growing number of younger Americans understand this.

4

The socially conservative lower middle class increasingly wants to be left alone. By lower middle class I refer to skilled workers, sales and service workers, and lower-level white collar workers with family incomes of about $25,000–$40,000. By socially conservative I mean those who see family and religion as the cornerstones of their lives. This group includes many of those who are most alienated from the public schools. They are appalled by the vulgarity they see on television and in the movies. They hate the idea of accepting handouts. They want their children to grow up to be hardworking, honest, and God-fearing. Their values are those of the dominant culture of the 1950s. They didn't change; the rest of the country did. They feel as if their way of life is under assault, and they have a point.

Their lives make a mockery of the line that "Americans say they want smaller government except when it comes to their own benefits." This group gets remarkably little from government. Its members are hardly ever on welfare or on the unemployment line. They are not rich enough to take advantage of tax breaks or powerful enough to get subsidies, but they make enough to pay serious taxes. Their neighborhoods are not affluent enough to enjoy the independence from government services that money can buy but not poor enough to qualify for the programs aimed at the poor. Their neighborhoods often abut high welfare and high crime areas, and as a result their public schools tend to be bad, and crime spills across into their streets. City services are as inefficient for them as for anyone else, and often worse—they haven't any political clout.

Just what does the government do for them that they

should fear losing? Social Security and Medicare? They pay enough in FICA and FICAMED to purchase more attractive annuities and insurance in the private sector. Some of their children qualify for government-sponsored college loans (but many could get those loans on their own if their tax rates were lower). The homeowners among them get a tax deduction for their mortgage (but often their net taxes would be just as low if their tax rates were lower). By and large this population pays for every nickel in benefits that it eventually gets, and then some.

Meanwhile government seems to be systematically siding with their antagonists. Violent criminals released onto the streets, condoms distributed in the schools, public housing projects a few blocks down the street—these are not just "issues" for the socially conservative lower middle class but ways in which government immediately affects their lives. Other things are mostly symbolic—the Supreme Court bans school prayer—but there are many such symbolic affronts, and they irritate like fingernails scraped along a blackboard.

Then, when these people want to do simple things to improve their lives—maybe enlarge their front porch, or join with their neighbors to put some play equipment in the corner park, or try to make some money working out of their home—they find that they must have the government's permission. They jump through bureaucratic hoops, spend time and money—and are often turned down. America's socially conservative lower middle class gives a great deal to government and gets mostly grief in return.

Historically America's socially conservative lower middle class was heavily Democratic. Many became Reagan Democrats in the 1980s but retained an underlying belief that government *could* be on their side again, as it had once seemed to be. That belief has been eroded to the point where many of them are now ready to respond positively to this simple and true statement about their circumstances: "You are no longer the beneficiaries of big government but its victims."

5

Americans do not want to give up government altogether. Everyone wants police protection, a fire department, an efficient court system, street lighting—the basics. But for much of the rest a fundamental shift is possible if political leaders will put the choice directly, honestly, and without escape hatches: "To get rid of big government, here are the things you will have to give up, just as everyone else will have to give up something. In return, you will get to keep about 90 percent of the money you earn and will be left alone to live your life as you and your family and neighbors see fit." It is a bargain that large numbers of Americans are ready to begin considering—tentatively and nervously at first, then more seriously.

Lived Freedom

THE PROPOSITION: *As the elites experience freedom in their own lives and see it denied to others, large changes become possible.*

Two groups of Americans—one already extremely influential, the other about to become extremely influential—live lives that are de facto free. Few of them think of it that way. As more of them come to understand what they are doing, they become vulnerable to this question: Why not extend freedom to everyone else as well?

1

The first group consists of the affluent baby boomers, now in their forties and early fifties, nearing the height of their national influence. Republican or Democrat, they are already buffered from many of the failings of government.

Where they live, crime is not high. If they live in a big city, they are likely to live in a high-rise with a private security force and shop in a neighborhood of stores and businesses that also employ private security forces. In the suburbs the affluent run their police forces to suit themselves and get excellent police protection as a result.

The garbage is picked up regularly for the affluent, by private services if necessary. For the affluent, public places defaced with graffiti and made unpleasant by the homeless are fleeting aspects of their lives, seen mostly through the car window. The affluent don't spend much time in such places.

The affluent send their children to good schools, and these schools pay attention to the concerns of the parents. If affluent parents aren't satisfied with the public schools, then their children go to private ones—it's taken for granted.

The affluent are little bothered by bureaucracies in their personal lives. They hire accountants to prepare their taxes. They hire people to take care of getting building permits and zoning variances and sometimes even to stand in line for the driver's license renewal or to take the car for its annual inspection. The affluent who run small businesses have to cope with the government, but those who work for large corporations are less bothered. Whole corporate departments are devoted to handling the regulations and paperwork.

The affluent have just about all the freedom of association they need. They increasingly hold jobs, or hire people for jobs, that are too senior to be affected by the government's employment regulations. They live in neighborhoods too expensive for all but a small fraction of the population to afford, thereby selecting out most of the people they would consider objectionable neighbors.

2

The ways in which the affluent buy themselves out of the system have been so visible that the phenomenon has acquired a label—"the secession of the successful." It is an important phenomenon because the group it involves is getting so large. Suppose we define *affluent* as beginning at an annual family income of more than $100,000. Such households constitute about 6 percent of American families, concentrated among the over-forty baby boomers. This group wields enormous influence on American life—economic, political, cultural, intellectual.

It is also a politically sophisticated population, and self-analytic to a fault. An increasing proportion of these people, liberals as well as conservatives, are aware of what they are doing. They know that they are using money to buy freedom from the laws they don't like.

When the secession of the successful began, many of them could rationalize their behavior: Government assistance for the poor, which most of them supported, would eventually make things better for everyone. But few hold that belief anymore. The American class system is looking more and more like an aristocratic hierarchy in which the privileged enjoy one relationship with government while the peasants must endure another, and many of the privileged know it. As this recognition spreads, there is reason to hope that many of the successful baby boomers can be made to feel embarrassment—perhaps even shame—and to modify their policy views on some key issues.

3

Now consider people in their twenties and thirties who are part of the ongoing computer/telecommunications revolution. For people who are at home with the technology, everything is changing—the way they conduct their vocations, their options about where to live, the means they use to interact with friends and colleagues around the world. Everything is in flux, and predictions are impossible. There is only one constant: Everything about this new way of life gives more power to individual human beings at the expense of power to centralized institutions.

This revolution has double-edged effects for the bottom of society but only positive effects for those who rise to the top. The people under forty who will come to political and economic dominance over the next two decades are becoming accustomed to an extraordinary degree of autonomy in their daily lives. Many of them take it for granted that they can work at home as easily as at the office. Of course they can tap into thousands of data bases at will, transact financial and business dealings internationally without intermediaries, conduct analyses on their own that would have required a large research team only a few years ago. There is nothing unusual about it to them—that's just the way their world is.

They also live in libertarian electronic worlds. The Internet has no government, no leader. It is still chaotic, developing the internal etiquette and shared conventions that will eventually provide a sufficient amount of order. This developmental process does not require coercion or the regulation of government. For those on the Internet "spontaneous order" is not a phrase invented by obscure economists; it is a living phenomenon, taking place before their eyes. For the successful under-forties this lived experience with a libertarian world is not threatening but rewarding, fascinating, and fun. The unregimented freedom of it is an integral part of the fun. This population, acquiring growing power in society, is potentially more sympathetic to freedom as an ideal than any other post–FDR generation.

This population is also easily irritated by government bungling. For the generations under forty, perhaps more vividly than for their technologically inept parents, the incompetencies of government are absurd. A city government that takes six months to fix a pothole because it can't track the reports of complaints? A federally run air traffic control system that still uses 1960s technology? The post–baby boomers understand how backward these bureaucracies are, and they are pragmatic enough to think about dumping incompetent institutions instead of trying to limp along with them.

4

The task is to talk to both generations, the affluent baby boomers and the technologically fluent post–baby boomers, about the connections between losses of different kinds of freedoms. The parent who wants to have control over where his child goes to school and the entrepreneur who wants to run his own business both want to make their own decisions about what is best for them. The government's attempt to censor what you choose to access on the Internet is of a piece with its attempts to make you wear a seat belt: Neither is any of its damned business. When a court holds that one person can have the value of his property taken from him without compensation and holds that another person does not have the right to hire whom he chooses, both people are being robbed.

For several decades the received wisdom among America's elites has been that we live in a complicated world, the Constitution is a living document that must be adapted to the times, and America's traditional ideas about individualism and freedom are outmoded. But the people who have recently come to dominance and those who will come to dominance in the new century are increasingly aware—or can be made aware—that freedom still works in their own lives and that they effectively exempt themselves from most of the laws that take freedom away from other people. As this awareness spreads, there is an opening for a simple message: Freedom works. You know that from your own life. Give it a chance to work for everyone else as well.

The Stuff of Life

THE PROPOSITION: *As people seek to reacquire control over the stuff of life, large changes become possible.*

Human beings are awake for about sixteen to eighteen hours every day. That time has to be filled up. Beginning in the 1960s and continuing to some extent today, large segments of American society tried to fill their days with career and amusements. Self-fulfillment was everything, defined in terms that gave short shrift to parenting and neighboring. It was the ideal period for government to centralize functions that families and neighborhoods had formerly filled, because the prevailing attitude, with the elites' confident endorsement, was "Good riddance." Families and neighborhoods hadn't done these tasks well enough. Who needed them, anyway?

And so we moved much of what I refer to as the *stuff of life*—being engaged with those around you in the core social roles of spouse, parent, son or daughter, friend, and neighbor—downtown, to the bureaucracies. This was the most important change in social policy during the last thirty years. Not the amount of money government spent. Not how much was wasted. Not even the ways in which government hurt those it intended to help. Ultimately the most important effect of government's metastasizing role was to strip daily life of much of the stuff of life. We turned over to the bureaucracies a large portion of the responsibility for feeding the hungry, succoring the sick, comforting the sad, nurturing the children, tending the elderly, and chastising the sinners.

For a while the new order seemed to be a reasonable sharing of responsibility. After all, those of us who were parents and wanted to nurture children had our own to take care of. Those who had the time and dedication to help in the community could find places to volunteer. Meanwhile those of us who didn't want to do these things could play our part by paying taxes.

There were two miscalculations in this approach.

1

The first miscalculation was to think that vital communities would continue to exist without having vital functions to perform. The policy makers thought in terms of discrete problems. Food stamps will take care of feeding the hungry, public housing programs will take care of people who need housing, Medicaid will pay for medical bills, and AFDC will give a cash income to single mothers. All these services will be supervised by the social workers. Meanwhile the policy makers apparently assumed that the neighbors would continue to keep an eye on each other's children, take a casserole next door when someone was laid up in bed, and help each other out in the hundred other undramatic ways that make up a functioning community.

It doesn't work that way. People keep an eye on each other's children because, in the first place, they know them. They know them because they are thrown together with their parents. They are thrown together with their parents to do things that have to get done around the neighborhood. They do these things for the most unsentimental of reasons: If they don't do them, no one else will.

Readers who are parents know how this process works.

You don't go to the Little League fund-raising supper because it will be fun. You don't make sure the homework is done tonight because that particular assignment is vital to your child's education. You don't drive your child to a music lesson or birthday party because you have nothing more interesting to do. You do these things because each one, trivial individually, is part of a larger process, the larger process is crucially important, and the individually trivial pieces of the process won't get done unless you do them.

The same is true of what we do as engaged members of communities. Life acquires texture not just from the hours one devotes to an activity but through an ongoing consciousness of engagement and responsibility. No, it is not required that everyone devote twenty hours a week to volunteer work. But you must have a sense that you are juggling your time and your energies so that you play your part in the little platoons to which you belong. The tasks involved in "playing your part" are often not fun. But you have to play your part, because the things that the community does have to get done. When that statement is no longer true—when government is not only willing to take most of the important functions out of the community's hands but even insists on doing so—people gradually drift away from the functions that remain.

The reason for restoring the stuff of life to communities is not so that every last person will be bludgeoned into doing his civic duty. In a free society there will be many who live aloof from their neighbors, and that choice is properly theirs. Little platoons do not require universal conscription. Rather, for most of us, being engaged in our community falls under the heading of retrospective satisfaction: things that we are glad we have done. The immediate reward for any one act may well be zero. The reward for the totality of many such activities—ones done by yourself and ones that you observe being done by others—is to broaden and deepen your relationships with the people around you. Lacking that sense of engagement with your little platoons in the stuff of life, life itself becomes a smooth, flat surface—shiny, perhaps, but two-dimensional.

2

The second miscalculation was to think that the geographic neighborhood is no longer a critical part of American life. The elites are especially myopic on this point. They look at their own lives and see very little loss in giving functions over to bureaucracies. For them, affluent and professionally successful, the neighborhood is often little more than the physical location of their house. Their little platoons are drawn from professional circles, people with shared intellectual interests, old school ties, and clubs, and are scattered around the city, the country, and increasingly, the world. But the elites are a small minority. For much of working-class and middle-class America the geographic neighborhood continues to be important. Friends are likely to live down the street. Engagements in social life are likely to be grounded in the neighborhood churches, lodges, service organizations, charities, and schools. I am not referring just to small-town America. It is true as well of working-class and middle-class neighborhoods in Brooklyn and San Diego.

Just as the little platoons of working-class and middle-class America tends to be grounded in the geographic community, so are many of the satisfactions of life. People in these platoons do not have the option of thinking well of themselves because they just got promoted to executive vice president or appeared on *Meet the Press.* If they are to reach old age able to look back with satisfaction on who they have been and what they have done, their primary sources of pride and satisfaction will be that they have been good spouses, parents, sons and daughters, friends, or neighbors.

These are not inferior sources of satisfaction. On the contrary: The affluent and successful also find themselves focusing on these core roles as they get older and regretting they didn't value them more when they were young. My point is simply that for a large part of the population the satisfactions of life *must* come from the core roles. When the government stripped neighborhoods of functions, the consequences were most devastating where the geographic neighborhood was most important.

3

There is a growing, still unfocused, recognition of what we as a society have inadvertently done. We haven't left enough important things to do for ourselves. It may seem an odd claim in an age when people are working longer hours than ever and magazines are filled with articles about stressed-out two-career families. But that is a reflection both of the problem and of our growing sense that it is a problem. People are asking themselves just why it is that both parents are working full time. To make more money? More money to do what? Why the obsessive hours to get a promotion? To what end?

Sometimes there is a legitimate answer: To make more money so that my family can have a decent standard of living. To get a promotion because I find my work rewarding, and a promotion will let me exercise my abilities more fully. But for a great many people the extra money does not make much difference in their standard of living, and the promotion does not increase the satisfaction they gain from their work. Instead, too often, the money is spent on minor amusements, and the promotion takes people away from the aspects of their job that they loved. And even at their best, amusements pall and the satisfaction of the job leaves empty spaces that need to be filled elsewhere.

This is the experience of individuals as they grow to maturity, and perhaps it can be the experience of an entire society. One explanation of why family and community have become so fashionable again in the 1990s is that a society that abruptly regressed to adolescence in the 1960s has finally grown up again.

That family and community have become fashionable is obvious to all. *Family values, community,* and *civil society* have become such catch phrases that they are in danger of being trivialized. But the basis for the reawakened interest in family and community is this deep and abiding reality: To live a satisfying life, you have to spend a goodly portion of your waking hours doing important things. "Important things" mean the stuff of life. More and more people want to have the stuff of life back in their hands.

Conclusion

FREE ECONOMIES teach us that predictions are confounded by human ingenuity. Go to the stacks of a library and read the articles from forty or fifty years ago in *Colliers* or *Popular Mechanics* predicting what the United States would be like in the year 2000. All they could imagine was extensions of the existing technology. Nobody could imagine the microprocessor. Go back and read the learned economists from the 1960s and 1970s who argued that IBM had to be broken up because of its monopolistic power over the computer market. There was no place in their world view for a couple of kids who would get together in a garage and revolutionize the industry. Freedom regularly makes ridiculous anyone who thinks he has figured out the limits of what is possible.

I have had to remember that lesson when thinking about politics. An eminent body of political theory beginning with *The Federalist* argues convincingly that the walls of limited government, once breached, cannot be rebuilt. Looking at the course of recent American history, it has been easy to conclude that the nation is on an inexorable downhill track—not economically or as a military power, but as a free society. On a pessimistic day I am still inclined to believe that within a few decades America will be a riven society of haves and have-nots where freedom is a perquisite of the rich while the poor get bread and circuses.

But just because theory says it should happen doesn't mean it will. Given a country where a fair amount of freedom still abides, trying to predict political futures is just as foolish as trying to predict technological futures. The forces for change I outlined in the last four chapters exist and are potent. We have seen in recent elections that political outsiders who are consistently committed to limited government can be elected to Congress. Sooner or later there will appear an attractive national figure for whom limited government is not one goal among many but the ideal to which he dedicates his political life. As these elements fall into place, the possibilities for reform are open-ended. How the political struggle will play out is beyond guessing. I assume that it will be more like MacArthur's Pacific campaign than Agincourt. But who knows?

Meanwhile we who believe in freedom and limited government must remember the essence of what we are about. It is easy to get caught up in the nuts and bolts of our complaints and our objectives. Cut taxes. Elect the right congressional candidate. Defeat the wrong Supreme Court nominee. Repeal a particularly objectionable law. Unless we step outside practical politics from time to time, we lose sight of the intensely idealistic vision that lies behind these specifics.

Libertarianism is a vision of how people should be able to live their lives—as individuals, striving to realize the best they have within them; together, cooperating for the common good without compulsion. It is a vision of how people may endow their lives with meaning—living according to their deepest beliefs and taking responsibility for the consequences of their actions.

We may honor that vision in the way we act in our own lives, whatever the political system may be. Human freedom has always had to depend first on the individual's understanding that he is the custodian of his life, no matter who tries to say otherwise.

We may honor that vision in politics—compromising when necessary on the terms of the legislation, but not compromising on the terms of debate. Of the many forces that will eventually reestablish limited government, the most powerful will be a renewed understanding that only freedom enables human beings to live fully human lives.

SOURCES AND ACKNOWLEDGMENTS

THE CLASSIC WORK that has most decisively affected my thinking is Adam Smith's *The Theory of Moral Sentiments,* with his better-known *Wealth of Nations* close behind. It is not necessary to read every word—Smith has long disquisitions on topics peculiar to eighteenth-century England—but Smith is a terrific read, brimming over with thought experiments and empirical observations on human social behavior, so perceptive that he is as much a founding father of sociology as of economics. Jerry Z. Muller recently published an excellent short analysis of Smith that will guide you to many of the best passages: *Adam Smith in His Time and Ours: Designing the Decent Society* (The Free Press, 1993).

Two other classic documents that reward study in the original are John Stuart Mill's *On Liberty,* for inspiration, and *The Federalist,* for its austere and compelling analysis of the dynamics of democratic government. Having touted *The Federalist,* I must also encourage you to dip into the anti-Federalist literature. Herbert J. Storing edited an excellent anthology, *The Anti-Federalist: Writings by the Opponents of the Constitution* (University of Chicago Press, 1981). The anti-Federalists lost the political war, but recent history has given them a right to say they told us so.

The contemporary works that most broadly shape this book are Robert Nozick's *Anarchy, State, and Utopia* (Basic Books, 1971) and Richard Epstein's *Takings: Private Property and the Power of Eminent Domain* (Harvard University Press, 1985), each a Promethean intellectual feat, endlessly fascinating to a reader who gives them the time they deserve. In the world of today's classical liberal scholarship, Epstein calls to mind John Kennedy's famous comment about Thomas Jefferson dining alone, for reasons that will become evident as I cite one Epstein book after another in the following pages.

Another contemporary book that has influenced my thinking is Mancur Olson's *The Logic of Collective Action: Public Goods and the Theory of Groups* (Harvard University Press, 1965). It is a depressing work, suggesting that without a war or economic collapse the polity will never get out of the box it has wedged itself into, but you will understand the dynamics of the expansive state much better after reading it. For more on the same topic see another modern classic, *The Calculus of Consent: Logical Foundations of Constitutional Democracy* (University of Michigan Press, 1962), by James M. Buchanan and Gordon Tullock.

Exemplary short works on classical liberal thought include Milton Friedman's *Capitalism and Freedom* (University of Chicago Press, 1962), Henry Hazlitt's *Economics in One Lesson* (Harper & Bros., 1946), and of course Friedrich Hayek's *The Road to Serfdom* (University of Chicago Press, 1944). For those who are more ambitious, the closest thing to the canonical text among the Austrian economists is Ludwig von Mises' *Human Action: A Treatise on Economics* (Yale University Press, 1949). It is exceedingly tough going, however. Mises' *Liberalism in the Classical Tradition* (Cobden Press, 1962), translated by Ralph Raico, is much more accessible. Among Hayek's full-scale works a good place to begin is *The Constitution of Liberty* (University of Chicago Press, 1960). An excellent short course in both theory and basic writings is David Boaz's companion set, *Libertarianism: A Primer* and *The Libertarian Reader: Classic and Contemporary Writings from Lao-tzu to Milton Friedman* (Free Press, 1997).

A question commonly asked of any libertarian is what he thinks of Ayn Rand. I devoured *The Fountainhead* and *Atlas Shrugged* during my teens and still reread favorite passages from time to time. But newcomers to this part of the political-philosophical spectrum should be warned that Ayn Rand's philosophy—objectivism—occupies a highly fortified position distinct from the classical liberal tradition and at outright odds with much in this book.

This short list of works that have most influenced this book barely begins the roster of great works undergirding classic liberal thought (I haven't even mentioned Hobbes, Locke, Hume, Jefferson, or, among the moderns, Murray Rothbard). Two catalogue-based distributors are excellent sources for titles that are hard to find in general bookstores: Laissez Faire Books in San Francisco, with a predominantly modern list, and Liberty Press in Indianapolis, which republishes long-out-of-print classics.

Some reading on specific topics in
What It Means to Be a Libertarian

In Part I: For an accessible but much more precise discussion of public goods and tort law than I give, see Richard Epstein's *Simple Rules for a Complex World* (Harvard University Press, 1995). For what went wrong with tort law, George Priest's "The Invention of Enterprise Liability: A Critical History of the Intellectual Foundations of Modern Tort Law" (*Journal of Legal Studies*, Vol. 14, no. 3, 1985, pp. 461–527) is superb. I also recommend two popular accounts—Peter Huber's *Liability: The Legal Revolution and Its Consequences* (Basic Books, 1988) and Walter Olson's *The Litigation Explosion: What Happened When America Unleashed the Lawsuit* (Dutton, 1991).

Much of Part I of the book—and the rest of *What It Means to Be a Libertarian*, for that matter—draws heavily from my *In Pursuit: Of Happiness and Good Government* (Simon & Schuster, 1988, now available from ICS Press), which is fully footnoted. The discussion of satisfaction and happiness is influenced by Aristotle's *Nichomachean Ethics*, one of the many books that are wasted on us as college sophomores; try reading it again as a grown-up. I owe much in the discussion of the Aristotelian principle to John Rawls, from his *A Theory of Justice* (Harvard University Press, 1971). On the broader issue of how human beings find enjoyment in life, I am indebted to Mihaly Csikscentmihalyi's *Beyond Boredom and Anxiety: The Experience of Play in Work and Games* (Jossey-Bass, 1982) and *Intrinsic Motivation and Self-Determination in Human Behavior* (Plenum Press, 1985) by Edward L. Deci and Richard M. Ryan. My discussion of satisfactions also owes much to Michael Walzer's treatment of self-esteem in *Spheres of Justice: A Defense of Pluralism and Equality* (Basic Books, 1983).

Turning to Part II: Trendlines have fascinated me ever since 1981, when I came across a retrospective calculation of the poverty trendline going back to 1947, showing that poverty decreased throughout the postwar period as rapidly as it did during the glory years of the War on Poverty. I subsequently included long-term trendlines involving major social and economic outcomes in two of my books, *Losing Ground: American Social Policy 1950–1980* (Basic Books, 1984) and, with Richard J. Herrnstein, *The Bell Curve: Intelligence and Class Structure in American Life* (The Free Press, 1994). For trendlines on the economy see Herbert Stein and Murray Foss, *The New Illustrated Guide to the American Economy* (AEI Press, 1995). For trendlines on the environment see the Environmental Protection Agency's *National Air Pollutant Emissions Trends, 1900–1992,* and the appendix in *The True State of the Planet* (The Free Press, 1995), edited by Ronald Bailey.

You do not need to depend on secondary sources for trendlines. Combine the Census Bureau's *Historical Statistics of the United States, Colonial Times to 1970* (Government Printing Office, 1975), still in print, with the annual *Statistical Abstract of the United States,* and in short order you can produce a trendline on any of dozens of outcomes that might interest you. For more detailed breakdowns go to the Census Bureau's annual publications on poverty and money income, the Bureau of Labor Statistics, annual publications on employment and occupations, the FBI's annual *Crime in the United States,* the National Center for Health Statistics' annual *Vital Statistics,* and the National Center for Educational Statistics' annual *Digest of Education Statistics.* Trendlines on the environment may be reconstructed from the Council on Environmental Quality's annual *Environmental Quality* and the Environmental Protection Agency's *National Air Quality and Emission Estimates.* All are available in any good university library and, increasingly, over the Internet.

The literature on regulation is as huge as the number of special interest groups affected by regulation would predict it to be. Much of it consists of congratulatory analyses by proponents of regulation about the number of lives and injuries saved. In none that I have read will you find cost-benefit analyses that take into account the effects of either self-regulation (the effects that individuals may capture unilaterally) or displacement (cutting off the evolution of nongovernmental systems). A good ongoing commentary on regulation from a skeptical standpoint is found in the magazine *Regulation.* For a recent scholarly collection of articles on cost-benefit analyses of regulation see *Risks, Costs, and Lives Saved: Getting Better Results from Regulation* (Oxford University Press-AEI Press, 1996), edited by Robert Hahn. But the real story about regulation is to be found in the trenches. The collection of articles in *Regulation and the Reagan Era: Politics, Bureaucracy and the Public Interest* (Homes and Meier, 1989), edited by Roger Meiners and Bruce Yandle, describes some of the bureaucratic infighting that makes deregulation so hard to accomplish. Richard Epstein's *Bargaining with the State* (Princeton University Press, 1993) dissects the often Kafkaesque, ultimately corrupt relationships between regulators and the regulated.

Much more good scholarship is needed regarding the role of the government in sustaining racial discrimination and the role of civil society in breaking down discrimination. Progress is being made—it is possible to find the occasional journal article—but huge gaps remain. One of the few major works is Richard Epstein's *Forbidden Grounds: The Case Against Employment Discrimination Laws* (Harvard University Press, 1992). Several excellent books about the damage done by strong affirmative action have been published in recent years. Clint Bolick's *Changing Course: Civil Rights at the Crossroads* (Transaction Books, 1988) was one of the first. A recent one is Terry Eastland's *Ending Affirmative Action: The Case for Colorblind Justice* (Basic Books, 1996).

Books on ways to fix education and health care seem to be published almost weekly. My own position deals much less with any particular reform than with this simple proposition: Neither education nor health care could have reached its present state without having been shielded from evolutionary pressures by the government. This point has two specific inspirations. I had been in favor of vouchers or tuition tax credits for many years, but mainly on the basis of equity (why not let poor parents do what the rich already do?) and as a means of recovering the ground lost by misguided educational reforms. Milton Friedman first made me think about the more powerful pragmatic reason for vouchers: Education must be drastically improved, not just brought back to where it used to be, and such improvement will happen only when the creativity of the market is unleashed. Regarding health care, Stephen Hyde, one of the early entrepreneurs in the development of Health Maintenance Organizations, first made me think about the reasons why routine health care should be cheap and getting cheaper, not expensive and getting more expensive. For analyses of the problems in education and health care and somewhat less radical prescriptions than I offer, see *Politics, Markets, and America's Schools* (Brookings Institution, 1988), by John E. Chubb and Terry M. Moe, and *Patient Power: Solving America's Health Care Crisis* (Cato Institute, 1992), by John C. Goodman and Gerald L. Musgrave.

The discussion of drugs is a revised version of an article I wrote for *The New Republic*, "How to Win the War on Drugs," published in the issue of May 21, 1990. The general proposition that people must be free to make decisions that may harm them is central to libertarian thought and discussed at length in virtually all its major texts.

Readers who are skeptical about my presentation on the environment should start slowly, with a book on a single issue, to get a sense of how wrong the conventional wisdom about the environment can be. Alston Chase's *Playing God in Yellowstone: The Destruction of America's First National Park* (The Atlantic Monthly Press, 1986) or *Visions Upon the Land: Man and Nature on the Western Range* (Island Press, 1992) by Karl Hess, Jr., would be good choices. An excellent one-volume, data-packed set of essays covering a wide variety of issues and accompanied by an extensive bibliography is *The True State of the Planet* (The Free Press, 1995), edited by Ronald Bailey. Two organizations that produce excellent work on the environment from a free-market perspective are The Competitive Enterprise Institute in Washington, D.C., and the Political Economy Research Center in Bozeman, Montana.

The chapter on ending the welfare state deals with topics that have preoccupied me for many years. The first works to read are Gertrude Himmelfarb's pair of volumes on nineteenth-century British thought—*The Idea of Poverty: England in the Early Industrial Age* (Knopf, 1984) and *Poverty and Compassion: The Moral Imagination of the Late Victorians* (Knopf, 1991). The embarrassing reality is that debates about welfare and human behavior, poverty and dignity, moral accountability and philanthropy, were all conducted with more intellectual sophistication and rigor by nineteenth-century thinkers than they are today. Combatants on all sides of today's debate will argue more thoughtfully if they have read Himmelfarb. For an account of America's traditions for dealing with distress see Marvin Olasky's *The Tragedy of American Compassion* (Regnery Gateway, 1992). My *Losing Ground:*

American Social Policy 1950–1980 (Basic Books, 1984) bears on more recent history.

Part III: I owe the idea about coalitions of people who want to be left alone to Grover Norquist, who heads Americans for Tax Reform. Robert Reich, Secretary of Labor as I write, originated the phrase *secession of the successful.* The chapter entitled "The Stuff of Life" draws from my discussion in the "Little Platoons" chapter of *In Pursuit.* It was only after writing *In Pursuit* that I discovered Karl Hess, Sr., who had written on the same topic much more eloquently. See, for example, his *Community Technology* (Harper & Row, 1979).

THE IDEA FOR *What It Means to Be a Libertarian* came from an invitation to be the keynote speaker at the twenty-fifth anniversary celebration of *Reason,* a leading magazine of libertarian thought. Writing the speech—parts of which survive in Part III—was liberating in more than one sense of the word and made me want to do more such writing. I had to put the idea aside for a few years while I finished another project, but when I finally got to work on it, the book indeed turned out to be a labor of love. Special thanks go to Manny Klausner, Bob Poole, and Virginia Postrel for the speaking invitation and for all they have done to put libertarian ideas on the public agenda.

Many other libertarian colleagues—upper-case, lower-case, and fellow travelers—have been of inestimable value to me for years. I will risk naming a few—David Boaz, Ed Crane, Richard Epstein, Bill Hammett, Tom Hazlett, Karl Hess, Greg Lindsay, P. J. O'Rourke, Dick Randolph, Fred Smith, Tom Sowell, Irwin Stelzer, Joan Taylor—knowing how many others could as easily be on the list. I haven't the temerity to call Milton Friedman a colleague, but his advice over the years has been as wise as his critiques have been acute.

On the other side of the fence, the strong Burkean cast to my discussion of little platoons and the roles of family, virtue, and tradition reflects my diffuse obligation to Bill Bennett, Bob Bork, Bill Buckley, George Gilder, Dick Herrnstein, Mike Horowitz, Charles Krauthammer, Michael Novak, Jim Wilson, and three of the remarkable Kristols—Bea, Irving, and Bill. Conservatives or neoconservatives all, they have deeply influenced my sensibilities regarding all matters political and civil, even as I have persisted to their bemusement in my libertarian ways. To be able to call them friends is one of my greatest blessings.

Some people were so important to me during the last two years that no list of acknowledgments would be complete without them. Chris DeMuth, president of the American Enterprise Institute, and Michael Joyce, president of the Bradley Foundation, demonstrated by example what the defense of intellectual freedom is all about. Among my many undaunted friends, Cita and Irwin Stelzer were the kind whom people write songs about. Narisara, Sarawan, Anna, and Bennett were loyal beyond the call of filial duty. Catherine was heroic.

CHARLES MURRAY
Burkittsville, Maryland
28 June 1996